# The
# Make-it-
# Merry
# Christmas
# Book

# The Make-it- Merry Christmas Book

## BY JEANNE LAMB O'NEILL

Drawings by Jeanne, Sean, and Cyn O'Neill
Photographs by Stephen Fay

William Morrow & Company, Inc.   New York

*For all kindergarteners over the age of five, especially my own two beloved* wunderkinder, *Sean and Cyn*

1 2 3 3 5 6 7 8 9 10

**Library of Congress Cataloging in Publication Data**

O'Neill, Jeanne Lamb.
 The make-it-merry Christmas book.

 Includes index.
 1. Christmas decorations.  2. Handicraft.
I.  Title.
TT900.C4053      745.59'41       77-3013
ISBN 0-688-03207-9

# Contents

# Introduction

Do you know how to turn an old ragpile sheet into an exquisite golden angel? Can you see your empty mayo jars as an heirloom candlestick someday? Have you ever made an antique picture frame out of plain old Monday-night macaroni? Or beautiful fake flowers out of your corn-on-the-cob?

These are just a few of the fabulous "somethings" that you can create out of "nothing"—out of ordinary household scraps that most people throw away. Before we're finished, you'll think twice before you give *anything* to Goodwill, not to mention the garbage man—tin cans, turkey wishbones, egg cartons, cracked plates, prune pits, candle stubs, old crayons, Christmas cards, and, yes, even toilet paper rolls. You'll also take a new beady-eyed look at many of the ordinary, everyday staples you have around the house—table salt, cornstarch, flour, wax paper, and Kleenex.

But above all, I hope this book will open your eyes when you're out of doors. The woods, fields, shores, and even city sidewalks are overflowing with Christmas makings more precious than any you could buy. Nature's treasures are yours for the picking, so gather ye pine cones, pods, and seashells while and where ye may. Fair warning: you'll sniff a back-to-nature flavor on more than one of these pages.

In fact, maybe that's what the whole book is about. It's a love letter to the good old days when there were no tinselly "Trim the Tree" shops, no snow-in-a-can, no artificial trees complete with phony balsam scent, no luxury gift wrap counters, no gift certificates, no $50 per 100 name-imprinted cards and no Santa Clauses on water skis, no Gift Buying Seminars (no kidding, "seminars"—to guide women through the strains and tensions of the holiday shopping season), and, definitely, no ringside seats at a *Playboy* centerfold shooting (Neiman-Marcus's best-selling catalogue item one year). It's an old-timey hymn to old-fashioned thrift, making do, retrenching, recycling, improvising, wiggling your imagination instead of waving your checkbook—in short, to making Christmas mean something again by making-it-yourself. (For good measure, there's a whole chapter on how to recycle your wrappings.)

Mind you, I'm not a crusader. You and I know that you either *are* a make-it-yourselfer, or you're not. I wouldn't even try to pry non-artsy-craftsies away from their credit cards. This book is solely for those kindred souls who think the best part of Christmas is the *nights before* Christmas—all those happy, hummy hours spent puttering in one's workshop (in most cases, the kitchen table).

Nor will I pretend that I'm an expert, a know-it-all authority on candlemaking, tinsmithing, bread-baking, and such. There are whole books on these subjects, if you're so inclined. The projects here are mostly things I've dreamed up, lucked into, or stumbled on without any know-how beforehand. They're a purely personal selection, and a mixed bag, indeed—everything from elegant velvet Saint Nicks to the simplest salt dough stars. Some ideas I've borrowed from friends, neighbors, and elementary school art teachers. Some are oldies-but-goodies that you may have missed, or lost the directions for. Most are gifts and decorations that you won't find anyplace else but here, because they're my own creations, if that isn't too big a word. In fact, many are my very first attempts, which I trust you'll find inspiring. (By all means, improvise, experiment, go on to bigger and better things!)

All (with an occasional rare exception for good cause) are here for the same reasons: they're made of humble, everyday materials that cost next to nothing; they can't be bought for love or money; they're quick, easy, and fun to do (no long-winded, headache-y directions, but, like all crafts worth doing, they do require *some* patience); and they look like a million bucks. Plus which, you'll find that many projects can be enjoyed not just at Christmas but throughout the year.

Of course, making it yourself is messy, more often than not. That's what's so soul-satisfying about it (you know why you have to add eggs to cake mixes, don't you?). To me, the gooier the wheat paste, the gloppier the salt dough, the gunkier the melted wax, the goopier the Elmer's, the better. I'd rather play with yucky linoleum paste than yummy chocolate frosting.

So, see for yourself what fabulous things you can make out of goo, glop, gunk, and goop. What's a spotless kitchen or a perfect manicure compared to the joys of a merry, messy, make-it-yourself Christmas?

# Glossary of Materials

There's nothing more frustrating to a budding artsy-craftsy than being told to use such-and-such when she's never even heard of such-and-such. Where should she go to look for it—hardware store, crafts shop, florist, drugstore, five-and-ten? What does it look like? How much does it cost?

As already noted, most of the materials used in this book are things that you already have around the house or can gather for free outdoors—rags, empty cans and jars, egg cartons, candle stubs—pine cones, pods, and shells. Others are ordinary grocery items, like cornstarch, nuts, salt, and macaroni. Still others, such as Elmer's glue, gold spray, glitter, and styrofoam, are familiar to all and available everywhere. But here is a guide to those goos and glops and other special materials that may be new to you. The price quoted is in most cases the highest going price at a standard non-discount store; smart shoppers may well find the materials for less. Needless to say, all prices are subject to change, and you know in which direction, but at least you'll have some idea what to expect.

## CANDLE SUPPLIES

### CANDLE WAX

With all the interest in candlemaking these days, you'll find paraffin almost everywhere—candle shops, hobby and crafts shops, art supply stores, even some department stores. At American Handicrafts (a nationwide craft supplier with more than 500 retail outlets), a 9-pound slab sells for $3.50. Me, I prefer household wax by Gulf or Esso from the supermarket. At 39¢ for a 1-pound box, it costs almost exactly the

Many materials are things found around the house.

Others are ordinary grocery items.

Candle wax from the supermarket

same as bulk wax (or $3.51 for 9 boxes), but the individual ¼-pound cakes or bars (like print butter) are so much easier to handle. *Ask* where they hide it in your supermarket—it can be elusive. And be sure to stock up before the big home-canning season.

### CANDLE DYE

Candle dye cake

Usually sold in little cakes for about 45¢ each. It comes in many good, true colors, but you can use your old wax crayons or candle stubs just as well. More vivid "mod" colors cost 69¢ each.

### CANDLE WICKS

Don't ruin a good candle with ordinary poor-burning string when proper wicking is so inexpensive. For 69¢ you can get 5 whole yards of thick candle wicking or 10 yards of thin wicking (I recommend the thick for most candles). Unfortunately, my favorite easy-to-use wire-core wicking has been banned because it releases lead into the air.

### WICK TABS

A wick tab

Little, pronged metal gadgets that hold your wick in place, and well worth 49¢ for a package of 24.

### SILICONE SPRAY

Makes it easier to release your candle from the mold. $1.89 for a 16-ounce can.

## CLEAR CAST (*See* Plastic Casting Supplies)

## CHEMICALS

Chemicals must be purchased from hobby shops.

All the books tell you to trot to the drugstore, but don't believe it. The only place I've found chemicals, such as those used for fire-starter cones, is in hobby shops—specifically those that have a Science Center or that carry chemistry sets. 1-ounce jars from Perfect cost 50¢ each.

## CORN HUSKS

Commercially prepared natural husks can be found in hobby and crafts shops, when corn is out of season. A cellophane pack by Craft World with about 10 dozen 6-inch-long husks of varying widths costs $1.19, or about 1¢ apiece. Craft World sells only to retailers but will steer you to the nearest outlet (433 Hahn Road, Westminster, Maryland 21157). Many shops run out of husks by early spring, but look for new shipments in August.

Natural corn husks can be bought in crafts shops.

## DRIED FLOWERS

Nobody's dried flowers can beat your own, but more and better commercially dried materials are available every year. Shop the florist's, department stores, boutiques, and import outlets such as Pier One. You can order boxes of bright, pretty mixed flowers by Eighteenth Century Bouquet Company from the Williamsburg Craft House, Williamsburg, Virginia 23185 (catalogue available). Or write the company at 53 State Street, Princeton, New Jersey 08540.

Other mail order sources include Floral Art, P.O. Box 394, Highland Station, Springfield, Massachusetts 01109 (catalogue); The Pod Happy Shop, 865 Third Street, St. Petersburg, Florida 33704; Boycan's Craft Supplies, P.O. Box 897, Sharon, Pennsylvania 16146 (catalogue 75¢).

Dried flowers are expensive to buy.

In New York City, some florists who specialize in dried materials are: Stephen Barany, 149 East 72nd Street; Ronaldo Maia, 27 East 67th Street; Ed Stiffler, 308 East 53rd Street; and George Cothran, 238 East 60th Street. If you're interested in enormous quantities or have an "in," the biggest dried-flower wholesaler in New York is Chingos and Sons, 818 Sixth Avenue near 28th Street. Others are Kervan, 119 West 28th Street, and Charles Lubin Company, 31 West 21st Street.

## FISHING LINE

One of the best ways to hang ornaments, mobiles, et cetera, because it's nearly invisible. Don't fret over diameter numbers and pound tests—just ask for the skinniest clear line at sporting goods stores that sell fishing equipment. A dispenser of 60 feet of line is usually about 35¢.

Fishing line for hanging ornaments

## FLORIST'S SUPPLIES

Most of these indispensable helpers used to be known only to florists and garden clubbers but are now widely available in crafts shops, garden centers, five-and-tens, and many hardware stores.

## FLORIST'S CLAY

A green-colored waterproof clay that sticks firmly to glass, pottery, or metal. It's used to anchor your pinholder to the container, among other things. When using, remember that everything must be absolutely bone-dry—the clay, the pinholder, the container, and your hands. Store opened or used clay in a sealed plastic bag to keep pliable. Most brands sell for about $1 for 1 pound. Be sure yours is tarnishproof.

## FLORIST'S TAPE

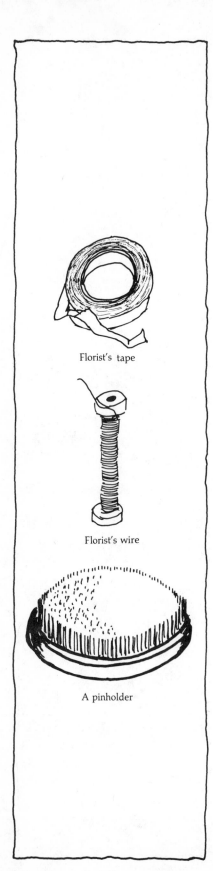

Florist's tape

Florist's wire

A pinholder

A thin, plastic, self-sealing ½-inch-wide tape used for wrapping fresh and wired flower stems. (The trick is to get a good tight start at the top and pull down hard with your left hand while twirling the tape with your right.) It comes in light and dark green, brown, and white for anywhere from 39¢ to 69¢ a 90-foot roll.

## FLORIST'S WIRE

A green-coated wire that comes in various gauges—the higher the number, the thinner the gauge—and is priced accordingly. For example, a cellophane pack of heavy #16 wire (about 25 pieces) costs about 59¢. A 150-foot spool of thin #24 wire costs $2 (mine's still going after almost daily use for ten years, so it's really not expensive).

## PINHOLDERS

Also called needle or needlepoint holders; the safest, surest, sturdiest flower holders going. The best are made of heavy green leaded metal with pins very close together. A Vogue model in the favorite 3-inch size costs about $3.

## OASIS

Another favorite flower-arranging aid made of spongy water-retaining polyfoam, usually sold by the block for about $1. Soak it well before fitting it into your container, and store used Oasis in a sealed plastic bag to keep it from drying out. Quickie and Filfast are similar products. For dried flowers, there's an ingenious new foam called Bar-Fast that comes pre-moistened; as it dries out it locks stems firmly in place.

Also about $1 a block. (From Filfast Corporation, Holliston, Massachusetts 01746.)

## STICKUM

A green-colored adhesive in tape form that *really* sticks, holds, and anchors almost anything to any clean, dry surface. Waterproof and tarnishproof, a 60-inch roll in dispenser sells for 59¢. (Beagle Manufacturing Company, Inc., 4377 Baldwin Avenue, El Monte, California 91731.) A similar sticky tape called Cling is colorless, which is handy for many projects. 98¢ a roll. (Floral Specialties Company, P.O. Box 3743, Birmingham, Alabama 35200.)

## WATERPROOF TAPE

This is no relation to florist's tape but a vinyl-coated pressure-sensitive tape that sticks to almost everything and is often used to secure Oasis in a container. Davee's Floral Tape costs $2 for 360 inches of ¾-inch tape; Oasis Waterproof Tape costs $3.95 for 60 yards of ½-inch tape.

# GESSO

A white pre-mixed plasterlike material used to prepare a surface for painting or gilding. American Handicrafts Folk Art Gesso is $2.25 for 1 liquid pint.

# GLYCERIN

A thick, colorless, liquid substance used for preserving fresh foliage. (To glycerinize leaves, slit and pound stem ends; stand in about 4 inches of 1 part glycerin to 2 parts water until solution reaches tips of the leaves, usually about 2 weeks.) Sold in drugstores, and expensive—$1.39 for 4 fluid ounces in one cut-rate drugstore. (Less costly anti-freeze solutions will sometimes work just as well.)

# GOLD WIRE

The thin braided gold wire recommended for tin can flowers and useful in many other ways is sold by American Handicrafts as Fantasy Film wire. 9-ounce spool, $1.95; 1½-ounce, 50¢.

Oasis, a flower-arranging aid

Cling, an adhesive

Gesso, used to prepare surfaces for painting

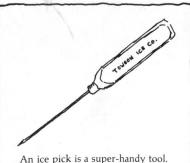

An ice pick is a super-handy tool.

Linoleum paste looks like chocolate frosting.

Mod Podge finish saves you time.

## ICE PICK

A number of other tools will do its various jobs, but a wooden-handled ice pick does them all, and better. Once you've splurged on this old-fashioned household staple (30¢ at our local ice house), you'll wonder how you ever got along without one.

## KRAFT PAPER

The strong, sturdy brown paper used for parcel post packages. Available at stationers in everything from 15¢ sheets to huge $36 bolts. Also available by the roll in 4 colors from East House Enterprises, 15 East 22nd Street, New York, New York 10010. $1.25 to $2 a roll.

## LAMINATING FILM

You'll find many other uses for these self-sealing clear plastic sheets besides making pressed flower bookmarks. Sold in hardware stores, stationery stores, five-and-tens, et cetera under many brand names. A cellophane pack of 2 large 9- by 12-inch sheets costs about $1.

## LINOLEUM PASTE

This is a thick, gooey, dark-brown substance that comes ready-mixed in the can; its many virtues make up for its less than perfumy odor. It starts setting up in seconds but remains workable for hours—perfect for macaroni trees, pine cone wreaths, and floral mini-wreaths. Sold in hardware and paint stores.

## MOD PODGE

A quickie glazing and texturing medium that is white in the jar but dries transparent. Popular with decoupage fans because it requires fewer coats to finish. $2.49 for 1 liquid pint (Connoisseur Studio Inc., 4006 Collins Lane, Louisville, Kentucky 40207).

## PAPIER-MÂCHÉ

This is not a store-bought product but simply the fancy name for a process you probably learned in kindergarten. All it involves is dipping torn strips of newspaper or paper toweling in some sort of paste (like wheat paste) and wrapping them mummy-style around a form. When thoroughly dry and hard, papier-mâché may be painted, sprayed, or shellacked. Actually, there *are* lazy man's papier-mâché products for sale now; one instant papier-mâché called Celluclay sells for $1.29 a pound, $4.95 for 5 pounds.

**PARAFFIN** (*See* Candle Supplies)

## PINE CONES

If you're a city girl with no cones underfoot to gather, or if you crave more exotic specimens, you'll find loose cones for sale (at absurd prices) at many garden centers and florist's shops. Or write to Western Tree Cones, 1925 Brooklane, Corvallis, Oregon 97730; Boycan's Craft Supplies, P.O. Box 897, Sharon, Pennsylvania 16146; or The Fir Tree, P.O. Box 130, Mi-Wuk, California 95346, for a catalogue or price list.

Pine cones are for free, but also for sale.

## PLASTIC BALLS

These marvelous take-apart clear plastic balls are sold in crafts shops and boutiques that specialize in handcrafted items, but may be hard to find. Write to G. A. Westphal Import Corporation, 34 West 27th Street, New York, New York 10001, for retail outlet nearest you—Westphal sells wholesale only. Plastic balls are #2789. 50¢ apiece with silver hanger.

## PLASTIC CASTING SUPPLIES

All of the following materials are from American Handicrafts, a nationwide craft supplier with more than 500 stores; or write for a catalogue (1011 Foch Street, Fort Worth, Texas 76107).

### CLEAR CAST

A clear, thick liquid casting resin that hardens quickly into transparent glasslike plastic (when catalyst is added). It's smelly and requires adequate ventilation—not recommended (by me) for children or apartment dwellers. Follow the directions on the can carefully. $3.95 a quart, $11.95 a gallon.

## CATALYST

The hardening agent necessary to make Clear Cast set up at room temperature; comes in a dropper-type plastic vial. 40¢ for ¼ ounce, 89¢ for 1 ounce.

## MARBLES

Bag of 85 clear Gem Tone marbles, 79¢.

## MOLD RELEASE

For quicker and easier release of casting from mold. 4 ounce jar, 79¢.

## MEASURING CUPS

Small throwaway graduated paper cups, 1¢ each.

## SPRAY GLAZE

Smooths out, shines, and hides imperfections in castings. 8-ounce spray can, $1.29.

## STIRRING STICKS

Wooden popsicle-type sticks, 2 for 1¢.

Spray Glaze shines plastic castings.

## PODS (*See* Pine Cones and Dried Flowers)

# POLYURETHANE VARNISH

A superior clear plastic finish with a super-durable, stain-resistant, mirrorlike high gloss. Many brands available in hardware and paint stores and departments. At Montgomery Ward ½ pint sells for $1.40.

Polyurethane varnish is best.

# RADIATOR PAINT

Not necessarily sold as such in your hardware or paint store; may be called aluminum paint or gold enamel, which sell for about $1 a half pint.

# SAND

Ordinary beach sand is all you really need for sand candles but, if that's not available, you can buy builder's sand very cheaply in lumber yards. At our local yard, 60 pounds in a plastic bag costs 90¢. Refills are even less (75¢), and in your own container you can get 100 pounds for 75¢. For drying flowers, you'll find children's sterilized play sand in hardware and toy stores for about $2 for 75 pounds. Or substitute a drying mixture of half cornmeal and half borax from the supermarket, or kitty litter.

## SILICONE SPRAY (*See* Candle Supplies)

## STITCH-WITCHERY

This is a magic two-sided iron-on bonding mesh that's sold in fabric stores and sewing departments. You can buy it by the yard for about $1, also in rolls of 1-inch-wide mesh for about $1.

## WELDIT CEMENT

A new crystal-clear cement that "cements anything to anything" and can often be substituted for more time-consuming epoxy glues (scratch metal surfaces first for a better bond). Sold in hardware stores, stationers, and five-and-tens. Woolworth's sells a 1½-ounce tube for 79¢.

## WHEAT PASTE

A grayish-white powder sold by the bag in hardware and paint stores; also sometimes called wallpaper paste. Mix it with water according to directions on the package. Rex brand is 79¢ for 1 pound; American Hardware is $1.55 for 2 pounds.

## WIRE CUTTERS

There are probably as many types and brands as there are hardware and variety stores—not to mention prices. I use Stanley's 7-inch All-Purpose Snips that sell for $6.05.

## YEAST

At your supermarket. Fleischmann's new Rapidmix active dry yeast costs 29¢ for three ¼-ounce packets.

Sand can be purchased at lumber yards.

Iron-on bonding mesh

Wheat paste is sold in hardware and paint stores.

Wire cutters are a good investment.

# 1

# Golden Angel

Golden angels, classic and adorned

I don't know where or how sheeting angels originated, but I saw *my* first angel more than ten years ago. She was shimmering exquisitely in an exquisitely appointed gift shop and wearing an exquisite $30 price tag. Little did I dream at the time what humble stuff she was made of—old sheets, brown paper bags, cardboard, wire, and wheat paste. Now that I know, I still think a sheeting angel is one of the most elegant Christmas adornments that you can create out of "nothing." (P.S. Just last Christmas I saw them selling for $50 and $60 in a major art museum's snooty shop.)

I learned how to make golden angels by word of mouth, which is how most bright new ideas sweep the country. Everybody on our lane was doing them, and I'm sure that thousands of women on other blocks

A Madonna can be made from the same basic form.

Another idea from the same pattern: a learned monk

Or a King

around the country were digging into their rag piles, too, that year. But by now there must be a whole new generation of make-it-yourselfers who have never seen sheeting angels. Or perhaps you missed them the first time around, or have mislaid your directions.

The directions given here are for a basic angel—simple, serene, unembellished (courtesy of Mrs. Robert S. [Peg] Knight). But don't be afraid to improvise and experiment. For instance, you can use a styrofoam cone or even an old bottle instead of a cardboard cone. You can coax your yarn into ringlets and swirly coiffures, braid it, or use un-angelic Titian-red yarn. You can handpaint a face on your angel, or add a halo or crown. Fold her hands in prayer or fling them out joyously. Or give her a harp, horn, or lyre to play. Use old "glass curtains" instead of sheets—and whatever fanciful trims you can find: braids, laces, ribbons. In fact, with the same pattern you can create a Madonna, a monk, the Three Kings, or any other Christmasy figure out of colorful fabric remnants—just skip the wings.

One suggestion: if this is your first angel, start with just *one.* Get the hang of dipping, folding, tucking and such before you go on to the next. Chances are, you'll be so smitten with the fruits of your labor (it's more like child's play), you'll want to make angels for everyone on your list. *Then* it's time for the assembly-line routine—not nearly as much fun but much more efficient.

## MATERIALS FOR GOLDEN ANGEL

12½-inch (radius) quarter-circle of cardboard for cone base
Cardboard for wings and base
Thin brown paper bags for "feathers" on wings
Piece of sheeting 18 by 30 inches for robe
Piece of sheeting 14 inches square for sleeves
22-inch length of #20 florist's wire for torso
Egg-shaped styrofoam ball for head
Paper toweling for papier-mâché face, neck, and hands
15 pieces of cotton yarn about 13 inches long for hair
Bag of wheat paste (follow directions for mixing)
Gold spray

### OPTIONAL

Assorted dressmaker trims
Cording for waist
Watercolors for painting face

# DIRECTIONS FOR GOLDEN ANGEL

### BASE

Form quarter circle of cardboard into cone. Staple and tape in place. (Figure 1)

### WINGS

Following pattern, cut out two wings. Cut slash on dotted line, overlap and staple (reverse second wing). Tear paper bags into pieces and dip in wheat paste. Push, pinch, and squish the pieces together to look like feathers (believe it or not, they *will* when sprayed). Cover one side of cardboard completely and allow to dry before covering other. When dry, spray gold and set aside. (Figure 2)

### TORSO

Bend wire in half. At center, measure down 1¾ inches and twist (this will be used to hold the head). Measure 1½ inches on either side and bend (to form shoulders). Bend again at 1½ inches to form elbows; twist wire ends into loops for hands. (Figure 3) Cover hands and neck with papier-mâché (strips of paper toweling dipped in wheat paste). Dry. Cut notches in cone, and set the torso in the notches.

### HEAD

Cover styrofoam egg with papier-mâché, gently smoothing out lines with your thumbs. Cover styrofoam completely or it will dissolve when sprayed. Dry.

### ROBE

First place cone on cardboard base for easier turning and drying. Fold 18- by 30-inch sheeting in half, then in half again. Take tiny snip out of corner, just big enough to fit over wire "neck." Dip sheeting in wheat paste and place on torso. Arrange in graceful folds, letting it trail over the cardboard. Turn under all raw edges after placing sleeves.

### SLEEVES

Fold 14-inch square sheeting diagonally and cut at fold. Dip each half in wheat paste and place largest corner at shoulder, underneath robe. Bring two ends to

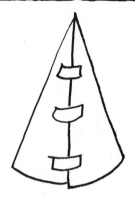

Figure 1: The cone provides the base for the angel.

Figure 2: The wing covered with paper "feathers"

Figure 3: The wire torso

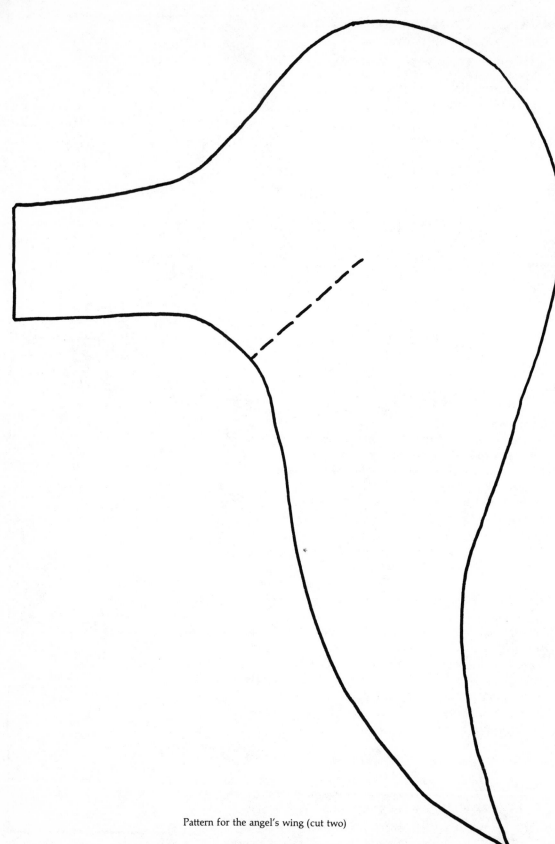

Pattern for the angel's wing (cut two)

the bottom, arranging in folds and turning under raw edges.

## HAIR

Place head on wire neck. Dip yarn in wheat paste and arrange on head one strand at a time. Twist into long coil down back (or do any other "do" you fancy).

## DRYING

Dry entire angel at least 24 hours.

## SPRAYING

Cut off excess cardboard from base. Make two slits with razor to insert wings at the shoulders. (Figure 4) Spray evenly with gold paint, one coat or two. Dry. Insert wings, concave side to the front, and I ask you— is that a seraph for sore eyes? The older your angel gets, of course, the more expensive and heirloom-y she'll look, but you can always respray if you like.

Figure 4: Cut two slits and insert wings.

A finished angel

# 2
# Macaroni Tree

Macaroni trees, plain and fancy

Back in the old whaling days, lonely New England sailors' wives used to spend hours fashioning seashells into intricate and beautiful designs. Today you can get much the same effect, in much less time, with macaroni from the supermarket. But don't stop with shellshaped macaroni—there are many other fascinating shapes on the shelves. There are bowknots, wheels, curls, twists, spirals, rings, cornucopias, fluted sticks, tubes, and, of course, elbows (if your usual market doesn't have a good assortment, try an Italian grocer).

You won't believe until you try it what a little gold paint can do for a bunch of pasta, but don't be discouraged in the making. To be sure, for a while your masterpiece will look like nothing more than pasty white blobs of spaghetti stuck into yucky brown glop, but gold spray will change all that—and soon! (Linoleum paste may smell bad but it dries overnight.) For a truly spectacular tree, sprinkle on glitter while you're spraying the pasta and add "ornaments" of seed pearls, glass beads, and other jewels. The shell shapes make good nesting places for beads, with a spot of Elmer's glue. Thrift shop necklaces are the best bet for jewels—unstring them and you'll have dazzle enough for several trees, all for a quarter or so. Save a real beauty for the top, or crown your tree with a gilded sweet gum ball. Make presents to strew at the base from odds and ends of gift paper taped to cardboard.

# MATERIALS FOR MACARONI TREE

| | |
|---|---|
| Assorted shapes of macaroni | Gold spray |
| Styrofoam cone | Glitter |
| Linoleum paste | Costume jewelry beads |
| Putty knife or other spreader | Elmer's glue |

# DIRECTIONS FOR MACARONI TREE

Spread linoleum paste onto styrofoam cone and let set briefly. That's the beauty of linoleum paste: It sets up fast but stays workable for hours. Add macaroni, either in a pre-planned design or willy-nilly, using larger shapes for first layer. Keep adding more paste and more macaroni until styrofoam is completely covered and tree looks "full." Allow to dry for 24 hours, then spray with gold paint and glitter. Add "ornaments." (P.S. Between holidays, store your tree in a sealed plastic bag with moth crystals to protect from mice and bugs.)

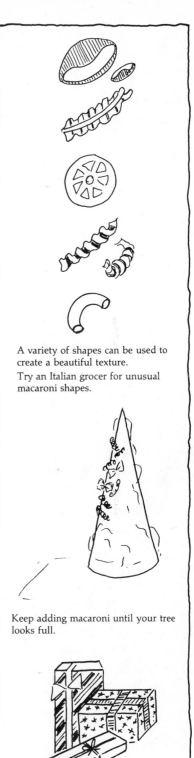

A variety of shapes can be used to create a beautiful texture.
Try an Italian grocer for unusual macaroni shapes.

Keep adding macaroni until your tree looks full.

Placing small presents under your tree makes a nice arrangement.

# 3
# Macaroni Mirror

A sugary-white seashell mirror made with macaroni

This rococo, gingerbread-y frame was inspired by an
18th-century seashell plaque in one of Massachusetts's
historic homes. The original was much more fussy-
Mary than this—in fact, the little lady who made it was
named Mary Edson. Each "flower" was formed from
dozens of teeny-tiny shells that were drilled and wired
together into roses, mums, and daisies before gluing
into place. By all means, try the real thing if you have
tons of souvenir seashells around and mountains of
old-fashioned patience. But, if not, on with the
macaroni!

The frame as shown takes only two kinds of
macaroni—shells and twists. One 1-pound box of each
(Mueller's costs 55¢) will make at least two frames.
Instead of gilding your macaroni, spray it with glossy

white enamel. For extra realism, touch up a few shells with brown watercolor. A coat of clear plastic will add extra sheen as well as protection. Macaroni creations are surprisingly tough and durable, but remember that they're only macaroni—you can't play football with them. (If you lose a smidgin here and there, you can always glue it back on with Elmer's.)

Obviously, you can use many more macaroni shapes and create many other designs. You can use the frame, *sans* mirror, as a picture frame.

## MATERIALS FOR MACARONI MIRROR

Macaroni shells and twists (or any shape you like)
Linoleum paste
Corrugated cardboard
Picture wire
White spray enamel
Mirror (cut to size at glazier's or hardware store)
Putty knife (or popsicle stick, Dixie spoon, or
    cardboard strip for spreading paste)

OPTIONAL

Mat knife (for cutting cardboard)
Old pie plate
Clear plastic spray
Watercolors
Navy beans and such (for flower centers)

## DIRECTIONS FOR MACARONI FRAME

Cut cardboard to desired size. The frame shown is 9 by 12 inches with a 2¼-inch border. Next wire the frame. Simply poke holes and knot the wire on the side facing up. It's much easier to do this now because the paste will secure the wire firmly when it dries. Be sure to allow room for the mirror to be taped on later.

Slather on a thick, thick layer of linoleum paste, with extra depth at the corners for a built-up effect and plenty of paste on the outside borders. While waiting a few minutes for the paste to set up, select rounded twists for the corners and straight twists for the border. Do border first, using an inverted throwaway pie plate to raise the frame so the paste won't stick to your work surface. Add an inner "gadroon" border with shells set sideways. Fill in entire area with shells and seashell "flowers."

Macaroni shells and twists were used for this mirror.

While you are working, place frame on raised surface to keep from sticking to work surface.

Wipe off excess paste from back; set aside to dry. Allow 48 hours to be absolutely sure frame is dried through before spraying. Spray with 4 to 5 coats of white paint, following directions on can. Tape mirror to back with masking tape and paint the back white for a finished look. (For frame shown, a 6- by 8-inch mirror was cut to order for $1. You don't really need such a good quality mirror, or, if you have an old mirror, adjust your frame to that size.)

Macaroni flowers:
Round shells, face up

Rosebud of broken twists

Skinny shells, face down

# 4

# Pine Cone Wreaths

An heirloom wreath is lavished with green and tan piñon cones lightly sprayed gold. Airy baby's breath, dried Queen Anne's lace, and chartreuse velvet bows add to its ethereal glamour.

The trouble with most pine cone wreaths that you see for sale is that they contain pine cones—period. They'd make Grinling Gibbons turn over in his Westminster Abbey grave. Gibbons was the 17th-century master woodcarver who was Sir Christopher Wren's pet, and a *proper* pine cone wreath should be just as intricately sculptured and elaborately designed as a Grinling Gibbons carving.

To make a proper wreath, you need not only pine cones of every size and description but also pods, nuts, seeds, and pits—at least one hundred separate goodies for an average-sized wreath. Just gathering your materials can take months. (Garden clubbers start in August to make their Christmas wreaths.) But, if time's afleeting, don't despair. You can order all kinds of

A proper wreath can become a family heirloom.

Work larger cones on the outer edge of the pegboards, smaller cones on the inside edge.

Create a glamorous plaque on a throwaway pie tin.

fascinating cones and pods by mail, and you can cheat with packaged nuts from the supermarket.

Basically, there are two ways to make a proper pine cone wreath—the "right" way and the jiffy-quick lazy girl's way. For years I sneered at the slouches who took the easy way out; to me, the measure of a good wreath was how many tedious hours and torn fingernails it took (you have to wire each piece individually and then wire it again to your frame). I hate to backslide, but the truth is that a wreath slapped together with linoleum paste looks *almost* as good to me, and probably just as gorgeous to everybody else. Your masterpiece may not endure unto infinity, but it will last long enough to suit most people. You'll find directions for both methods here (but do resolve to take the hard path of virtue *next* year).

## MATERIALS FOR WIRED WREATH

Tree cones of all kinds (pine, hemlock, cedar, larch, piñon, spruce, redwood, sequoia, cypress, etc.)
Other materials (sweet gum balls, horse chestnuts, acorns, nuts of all kinds, peach pits, prune seeds, cotton pods, eucalyptus pods, beech pods, etc.)
Pegboard ring, cut to size at lumber yard (wreaths shown measure 14 inches at outer diameter, 7 inches at inner diameter)
Wire cutters
Electric drill
Florist's wire, #22 or #24
Clear plastic spray
Pliers

### OPTIONAL

Artificial lady apples or other fruit
Baby's breath or other dried flowers
Velvet ribbon
Gold spray
Cotton felt, for backing

## DIRECTIONS FOR WIRED WREATH

Gather materials. The best time to collect fallen cones and pods is in the early fall before they become dark, weathered, or damaged. For hard-to-find specimens such as deodar roses, piñon cones and eucalyptus pods, see mail order sources in Glossary of Materials, page 1.

Rinse dirty cones quickly under hose or faucet spray. To dry cones and open up their scales, place on aluminum foil in a warm (150-degree) oven. Or pre-heat oven to 250 degrees and then turn off. Length of drying time depends on wetness of cones. Another method of cleaning cones is to soak them overnight in a bucket of water. For prolonged drying, cover with damp newspapers to keep cones from overbrowning.

When cones are dry, slice some into "flowers" with wire cutters. The cut ends will look like single-petaled flowers, the tips like chubbier blossoms.

Nuts and acorns must also be pre-baked to kill any lurking wildlife. Before baking, drill holes for wiring with electric drill.

Cones are easily wired by twisting thin florist's wire between the scales at the base. Wire each piece separately before you start to assemble your wreath. Group small cones, nuts, and acorns into clusters. Also, before you start, drill still more holes into the pegboard ring—remember, you have hundreds of pieces to wire on.

Next, plan your design, starting with the larger whole cones first. You'll find that an outer ring of overlapping look-alike cones, plus an inner ring of smaller cones, works best. (The large wreath shown is ringed with white pine cones on the outside, loblolly cones on the inside.) Keep adding materials and building up your wreath until every last fat, chunky inch is filled.

Use a pair of pliers to tighten your wires. As you go along, new pieces can be wired in back to already fastened wires. When you get to the final pieces, it will help enormously to prop your work on an easel so that light shines through the pegboard holes.

Now it's time to spray. Use several coats of clear plastic to polish and preserve your wreath. Believe me, when you finally behold your masterpiece in all its rich, glossy, mahogany-brown glory, you won't regret a minute of your toil and trouble.

Next come the finishing touches. Tie off and trim with wire cutters the excess wires in back, leaving a sturdy loop for hanging. Glue on a circle of felt to hide the jungle of wires and to protect your wall or door. Add trims—fruits, velvet bows, sprigs of dried flowers—or a *very light* dusting of gold spray. Of course, minus Christmasy frills, your wreath can hang proudly all year long. If you store it, in a tightly sealed plastic bag, be sure to add a handful of mothballs.

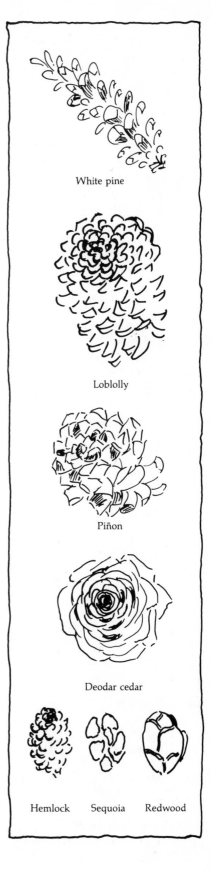

White pine

Loblolly

Piñon

Deodar cedar

Hemlock    Sequoia    Redwood

Cotton pod

Eucalyptus

Sweet gum ball

Beechnut

Douglas fir

Acorn

Casuarina

White pine "flower"

## MATERIALS FOR EASY LINOLEUM PASTE WREATH

Cones and pods, as for the wired wreath
Ring base (cut from solid plywood at the lumber yard
  or ordinary corrugated cardboard at home)
Linoleum paste
Wire, for hanging
Clear plastic or gold spray

## DIRECTIONS FOR LINOLEUM PASTE WREATH

Attach wire for hanging to plywood base. Spread a thick layer of linoleum paste on base and proceed with your design as in wired wreath, placing larger cones first. Dip additional pieces in paste as needed. Luckily, linoleum paste dries a dark brown, almost the color of pine cones, so you don't have to fuss and fret. Set finished wreath aside to dry for at least 24 hours before spraying.

Spray with several coats of clear plastic. Or gold. I wouldn't dream of burying a meticulously wired wreath under a heavy-handed coat of gold, but in this case, why not? The effect is marvelously opulent, Victorian, and, to be sure, Christmasy—great for quickie wreaths for friends or the church bazaar. For an even jiffier project, try a small gilded 8-inch or 10-inch solid plaque. (You can work these on ordinary throwaway pie plates.)

Use a wreath as an instant
centerpiece with a chunky candle.

(Top) Sturdy wired wreath has hung outdoors for many years, framed with fresh greens. Red velvet bows and gilded deodar cedar "roses" are festive extras. (Bottom) Hundreds of cones, nuts, and pods decorate a chunky wired wreath. Tiny red lady apples and clusters of rosy pistachios brighten it for a kitchen wall.

# 5
# Basket of Pine Cone "Flowers"

Two unusual arrangements of pine cone "flowers"

By now, you know that Christmas doesn't have to be all red-and-green or silver-and-gold. In fact, one of the biggest colors these back-to-nature days is brown. More and more of the country's snootiest florists are turning out enchanting little holiday decorations in earthy browns and natural beiges. Of course, there's nothing down-to-earth about their prices. Even the tiniest burlap bag of ordinary cones and a few dried posies can cost $25 on Manhattan's swanky East Side. Can you imagine what you'd pay for a beautiful, bountiful basketful of handmade, one-of-a-kind pine cone "flowers"?

Loblolly cone slices

Piñon cone slices

I can't even guess at the price because, thanks be, pine cone flowers are still pretty much of a garden club secret. The one and only time I've seen them for sale they were tagged at a ridiculous $1.25 per stem—and in a bargain-priced import outlet at that. "Ridiculous," because the cones are free and the making is no trick at all.

How do you turn a pine cone into a flower? Simply by slicing it in half. I won't say it's as easy as cutting into a ripe tomato, but it isn't as hard as chopping down an oak tree, either. And there's no end to the fascinating blossoms you can create. Many cones, such as the white pine, will yield two, three, or more different kinds of flowers (you saw a white pine "slice" on page 25). The sliced section of a loblolly pine cone looks like a dahlia; the base looks like a mum; and the tip, a dainty cornflower perhaps.

You don't even have to slice Western piñon cones—they're so pretty and flowery at both ends, your only problem is deciding which end to use. But the "slice" is nice, too. Probably the fairest flower of all comes from the deodar cedar—just as is, the cone is an absolutely perfect rose (see page 25). Of course, tiny cones need no surgery to serve as buds in your arrangements. Try tucking in hemlock, redwood, and sequoia cones (oddly enough, the smallest cones seem to come from the biggest trees).

Cones are yours for the picking, anywhere and everywhere, but be sure to keep your eyes open on vacation and weekend trips. I've found loblollies on the grounds of the Williamsburg Inn, acorns on the rolling slopes of Arlington Cemetery, and wee casuarinas on the beaches of Bermuda (you can still see the pink sand between the scales). Your own finds are better than the most exotic cones and pods from mail-order houses. But don't forget that even the most humdrum cones can be turned into fantastic blooms by adding other materials. Shimmery white petals of honesty or money plant (lunaria) can be tucked between the scales of white pine and loblolly flowers. Try tulip tree pods, pressed zinnia petals, rose hips—anything you come across in your gatherings. The ideas here are just the beginning of what you can do with pine cones and a little imagination.

You can also give your cones a new look with a few splashes of shiny white paint. Or pot a whole arrangement of painted pine cone flowers. The bright-eyed bouquet in the photograph is in shades of light blue, dark blue, and white acrylic paint. The stems are stuck into styrofoam in a navy-and-white polka dot china bowl with grosgrain bow to match.

## MATERIALS FOR BASKET OF PINE CONE FLOWERS

Cones (white pine, loblolly, piñon, hemlock, Douglas
     fir, deodar cedar)
Wire cutters
Thin florist's wire, #22 or #24
Heavy florist's wire, #16
Florist's tape, brown
Waterproof florist's tape
White enamel paint
Honesty (lunaria)
Baby's breath
Oasis or styrofoam
Clear plastic spray
Basket
Ribbon

## DIRECTIONS FOR BASKET OF PINE CONE FLOWERS

Weight basket with stones or pebbles before inserting
styrofoam block. Secure styrofoam to basket with
crisscrosses of waterproof tape. To camouflage
styrofoam, add a few whole white pine cones before
you insert your flowers and as needed afterwards.

Follow directions for cleaning and baking cones as
described in section on wreaths. (See page 25.) To slice
cones into flowers, slip sharp wire cutters between the
scales and press down hard. Thick cones may require
several cuts from different angles. To wire flowers,
wind thin florist's wire (#22) around scales at base of
cone; pull down and twist. Attach wire ends to heavy
wire (#16) stem with florist's tape. "Leaves" may be
added by taping on the single scales that will probably
drop off when slicing. Add white touches to flowers
with a small paint brush. Tuck honesty petals between
scales of cone flowers, with a dab of Elmer's glue to
keep them in place.

Arrange finished "flowers" and "buds" in basket
and fill in with baby's breath. Finish off with a pretty
brown-and-white gingham bow. Spray entire
arrangement—basket, bow, and all—with several coats
of clear plastic. (P.S. Garden clubbers don't *tie* bows;
they wire them. Simply loop your ribbon over and
over again, squeeze together tightly in the middle, and
secure with wire. The wire makes it easy to attach
your bow to the basket, or you can fasten it to a stick
to be inserted in the styrofoam.)

Honesty petals glued to cone

Wire cone flower with #22 florist's
wire: attach to stem made from #16
florist's wire.

Make leaves by attaching single
scales with tape.

A bow wired the garden club way

# 6
# Basket of Kindling Cones

Collecting pine cones is something like eating peanuts—it's hard to stop once you start. Before too long, you'll end up like every other pine cone picker I know—with a whole basement full of prickly treasures that you have to hide away from your husband, if not the fire inspector. Here's an elegant way to get rid of hundreds of them at a clip—especially all those squashed, dirty, and moth-eaten cones that you didn't want anyway.

Treat them with chemicals and use them to add a rainbow of blazing color to your cozy holiday fires. While you're at it, why not spray them gleaming gold and shower them with multi-colored sequins and glitter? What family wouldn't love a basket of

A basket of kindling cones with recycled package and nature flowers

glamorous, sexy fire-starter cones on the hearth—even if they don't own a white bearskin rug? For multiple gifting, simply pile the cones into shiny plastic bags tied with a gay ribbon. For a special present, or for your own hearth, heap the cones into a handsome basket swathed in bright plaid taffeta ribbon. (Cut your own ribbon with pinking shears from the same fabric used for wrapping a special package. The trim is a flower made from corn husks.)

Make a terrific present—or bazaar bauble—by piling kindling cones into a plastic bag tied with a pretty bow.

## MATERIALS FOR KINDLING CONES

Chemicals
    Sodium chloride (yellow flame)
    Borax (light green)
    Calcium chloride (orange)
    Copper nitrate or sulphate (emerald)
    Copper chloride (blue)
    Lithium chloride (purple)
    Potassium chloride (violet)
    Strontium chloride or nitrate (red)
    Barium nitrate (apple green)
Glue or paraffin
Gold spray
Glitter
Sequins

## DIRECTIONS FOR KINDLING CONES

The chemicals can be bought in hobby shops. Sodium chloride is ordinary tablet salt. Calcium chloride is also used for ice and dust control on the highways. If you have trouble obtaining the chemicals, or are just plain lazy, skip the first step. Untreated cones are fine for kindling, too.

Dip cones in melted paraffin or roll in Elmer's glue. While still wet, sprinkle immediately with chemicals. Let dry completely. Spray gold, and dust with sequins and glitter. Place layers of newspaper under the cones to catch the loose particles. (These particles can be reused.)

### ALTERNATE METHOD

Mix 1 pound chemical with 1 gallon water in plastic bucket. Place cones in mesh bag and weight with brick. Soak 10 to 15 minutes. Dry overnight on newspaper. Cones may then be sprayed gold and sprinkled with glitter and sequins.

# 7
# Miniature Wreaths

Mini-wreaths can hang on your tree or wall, or be used as candle bobeches.

There's no law against picking up other people's bright ideas while you're doing your Christmas browsing. Unfortunately, the pickings are pretty lean some years. Even in the most "unusual" boutiques everything begins to look alike after a while. I almost missed this shy little mini-wreath in the crowd of gaudy, assembly-line trinkets around it—and kept right on walking when I saw the $4 price tag. Four dollars for a handful of common-as-dirt pine cones and a smitch of tawdry tinsel? But, of course, I peeked at the mechanics and hurried home to try my own.

My mini-wreaths are heavy on dried flowers. If you're light in that department, you'll have to settle for store-bought strawflowers or starflowers. But here's how to dry your own posies for *next* Christmas. Simply pick them at their freshest and driest (in the middle of a sunny day); remove the leaves; bury them in dry sand for 10 days or so. Despite all the long-winded books on the subject (including my own *Flower Arranging Without Flowers*), that's really all you need to know. Store your flowers in sealed plastic bags till ready to use. Button zinnias, "Lemon Drop" marigolds, and black-eyed Susans turn out extra perky and are practically foolproof. You can dry rose petals simply by strewing them on a window screen (pink is best; red dries almost black).

So far as the other materials used, please don't think that these are rare and exotic treasures that only a gung ho horticulturist and flower arranger could have on hand. Pine cones and pods are yours for the picking everywhere—all you have to do is bend over or reach up. You can order more unusual species by mail (see Glossary). And anybody can come up with peach pits and pistachios.

Again, you'll find good old linoleum paste a joy to work with and a great timesaver. You can whisk through a small wreath in 10 to 15 minutes. My most elaborate effort took all of half an hour, including spraying and glittering the cones and pulling apart the "petals." To me, that's not too much time to lavish on a hand-made present—you'd spend that long racking your brain in a department store, not to mention standing in line to be waited on.

Mini-mini-wreaths are light enough to hang on the tree. Larger wreaths, of six inches or so, make enchanting wall decorations, especially in the kitchen, family room, or bathroom. Or use one as a candle bobeche on a small living room table. A string of them could solve your centerpiece problems.

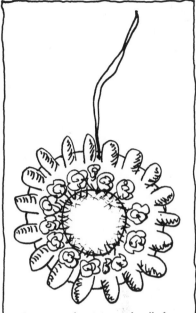

Even a simple mini-wreath sells for $4.

To dry flowers, cover the petals completely and carefully with sand. An old shoe box works fine.

Mini-wreaths make beautiful bobeches.

To make your work easier, perch your wreath on a tin can.

## MATERIALS FOR MINI-WREATHS

Cardboard, heavy or medium weight
Linoleum paste
String or wire, for hanging
Small cones, nuts, and pods
Pistachio shells
Prune or peach pits
Dried flowers
Jewels and other trims

## DIRECTIONS FOR MINI-WREATHS

Cut a ring 3½ to 4 inches in diameter out of cardboard. Poke hanging hole and insert wire. Slather on linoleum paste; let set briefly before adding materials. Spread paste with a piece of cardboard or Dixie spoon to save on clean-up. Perch wreath on a tin can to make working easier. Add materials as described in individual wreaths, or make up your own fancy-free designs. When wreath is thoroughly dry, paint the back red, green, or whatever. It's a nice idea to date your wreath and identify the materials used—and add a "Love, _____" if it's a gift. Store wreaths in a sealed plastic bag with mothballs.

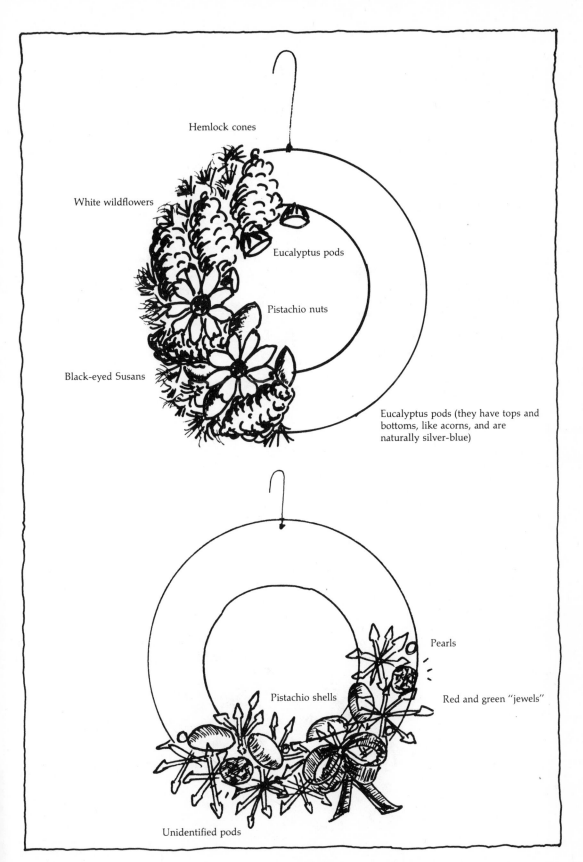

Hemlock cones

White wildflowers

Eucalyptus pods

Pistachio nuts

Black-eyed Susans

Eucalyptus pods (they have tops and bottoms, like acorns, and are naturally silver-blue)

Pearls

Pistachio shells

Red and green "jewels"

Unidentified pods

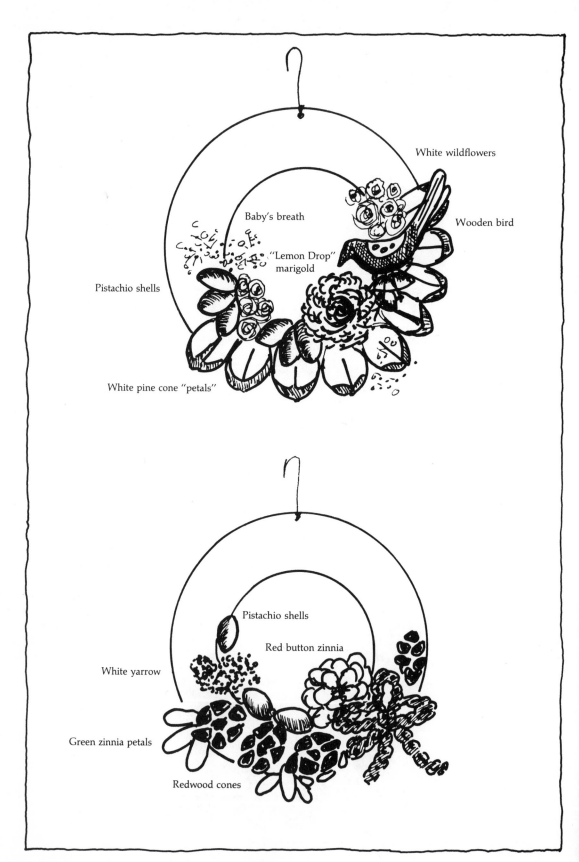

White wildflowers

Baby's breath

Wooden bird

"Lemon Drop" marigold

Pistachio shells

White pine cone "petals"

Pistachio shells

Red button zinnia

White yarrow

Green zinnia petals

Redwood cones

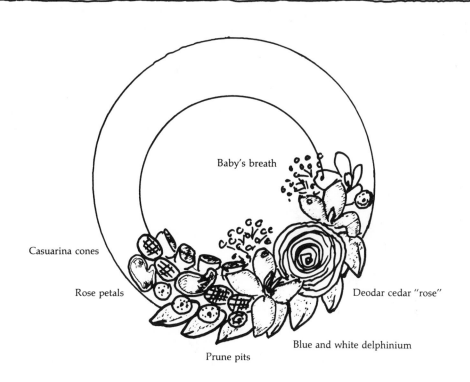

Baby's breath

Casuarina cones

Rose petals

Deodar cedar "rose"

Prune pits

Blue and white delphinium

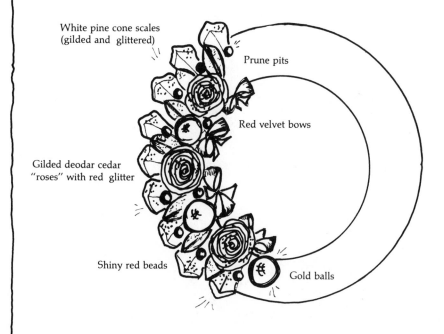

White pine cone scales
(gilded and glittered)

Prune pits

Red velvet bows

Gilded deodar cedar
"roses" with red glitter

Shiny red beads

Gold balls

# 8
# Dried Flower Notepaper

Pressing flowers is such a simple-Simon business that I'm always looking for something new to do with my pansies and buttercups—*anything* but another pretty-poo picture on gold-framed velvet. I learned this trick from a delightful local shop called The Flower Patch—elegant, airy stationery made from nothing more than facial tissue, wax paper, Elmer's glue, and a smattering of pressed posies. Happily (and rarely enough these craftsy days), I haven't come across it anyplace else since.

Elegant dried flower stationery is made with facial tissue.

This may be my favorite project in the book. To me, dried flower notepaper has all the elements of the perfect Christmas make-it-yourself. It's different, but not way out. It's pretty to look at, but not foolish and impractical. It costs next to nothing, but looks expensive as sin. Best of all, it's quick and easy to make, but looks like the most devoted, time-consuming labor of love.

The directions may put you off at first. Surely, you can't drag a paintbrush dripping with sticky Elmer's glue across flimsy *one-ply* facial tissue? Oh, yes, you can! So gather your supplies, pour a cup of coffee, and get ready to leave all cares behind. This one is *really* relaxing. (The laminated plastic bookmark is included here because it's even quicker and easier.)

A word about pressing flowers, in case you're not already a confirmed flower-drier. Pressing is the easiest method of all to preserve flowers. You don't need to be an expert or to make a big all-day production out of it. Press just a few flowers at a time, as they come into bloom and reach their peak of perfection. It takes only minutes, in between kitchen chores or gin-and-tonics, to "put up" a few dozen pansies or buttercups. Drop them between sections of newspaper, and weight with heavy books or slip them under the rug. Label and date them. Most flowers will be ready to use in a few days, or you can forget them for weeks or months. (Pressing flowers in the summer is sort of like planting bulbs in the fall, but the rewards for your forethought are swifter.) Of course, if it's already November, you're out of luck this Christmas, but get busy *next* summer. (You may luck into pressed flowers at some of the dried flower resources listed in the Glossary.)

Be sure to press special-occasion florist's flowers, too. Your creations will have more meaning with blooms from an anniversary or birthday bouquet. Gather leaves and wildflowers when you're on vacation—they're one of the smallest, *flattest* souvenirs you can carry home. Never come home from anywhere empty-handed—you never know when your pressings might come in handy. While working on this chapter, I came upon some pressed ivy I'd plucked from our son's hallowed Ivy League walls. Just in time for graduation, lucky kid. (Never mind—bookmarks don't obsolesce like Corvettes.)

Then again, you don't need prize specimens for your notepaper—use anything you can lay your hands on. Even in the dead of winter, there are weeds, grasses, and greens to be picked. How about parsley from your refrigerator, snitchings from a pet fern, or

1 TBSP ELMER'S GLUE
3 TBSPS WATER

Simply paint with a solution of Elmer's glue.

Press flowers in old newspapers . . .

BERMUDA THIS WEEK

. . . or inside magazines.

A bookmark made with ivy from Princeton

Try drying snippets from your windowsill herb garden.

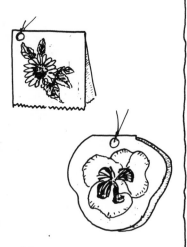

Gift enclosure tags can be made super-easily by the same process.

For presents, package several sheets in a clear plastic bag tied with a bow.

snippets from the windowsill herb garden in your city apartment?

You'll probably start with standard size folded notes (about 5 by 8 inches) and single sheets (about 8 by 10 inches), because that's the size of your tissue. But try slim-line notes, half-notes, and gift enclosure tags, too. Cut some tags into circles or pansy shapes. One simple design in the top corner of your paper is all you really need, but if you get carried away with an all-over masterpiece, slip a sheet of plain white paper inside to write on. In fact, I recommend this for all your folded notes. You *can* write on waxed and glued papers, but it's sometimes hard going. Besides, a white lining shows off your flowers more.

Actually, most of your friends will never use their elegant, one-of-a-kind stationery anyway. If you're the practical sort, stick to simple designs and provide a generous number of sheets to encourage them. Gifts that sit in the desk drawer are no good to anybody. On the other hand, you might want to sign and date an especially elaborate effort, in case it winds up in a frame.

Package your gift paper in recycled stationery boxes or Christmas card boxes with see-through lids; cover them with glued-on gift wrap. Or use a clear plastic bag. In fact, this crinkly flowered tissue makes a lovely wrapping in itself for small, special presents (the daffodil paper in the "Recycled Wrappings" chapter is a variation of same).

## MATERIALS FOR DRIED FLOWER NOTEPAPER

Pressed flowers
Facial tissue (Scott's "Calypso" comes four colors to the box; 200 two-ply tissues for 49¢)
Wax paper
Elmer's glue
Soft artist's brush, ½ to 1 inch wide
Aluminum foil
Tweezers
Pinking shears (optional)

## DIRECTIONS FOR DRIED FLOWER NOTEPAPER

Cut a piece of wax paper slightly larger than an unfolded piece of tissue. For folded notes, crease wax paper first to guide you in placing design, then unfold.

42

Place on aluminum foil and coat with 1 part Elmer's glue to 3 parts water. Position flowers with tweezers. Don't fret about pre-planning your design—you can push and slide the flowers around and change your mind a dozen times.

Lay single-ply tissue on top; brush again with glue. The trick is to cover the whole surface the first time; repeated brushing *will* tear the tissue. Set aside to dry. To prevent paper from sticking to foil, remove from foil in about 1 hour and finish drying on wax paper. Or, when paper is dry, trim off any stuck borders.

Cut dried paper to size. Use a ruler to draw your cutting lines—it's harder to cut straight than you think. Pink edges if desired. Save the foil for next time; keep leftover glue usable with plastic cover; wash out brush promptly. Press notepaper under heavy books for a finished look.

## ENVELOPES

It's a nice gesture to include envelopes, either bought or made, with your notepaper. To make envelope, cut away shaded areas. Fold side flaps in, bottom flap up. (Trim bottom flap away from fold of top flap.) Glue bottom flap to side flaps.

## BOOKMARK

### MATERIALS FOR BOOKMARK

Plastic laminating film
Pressed flowers
Tweezers
String, cord, or ribbon

### DIRECTIONS FOR BOOKMARK

Cut two matching plastic strips about 1½ by 8 inches. Peel coating off one; drop pressed material in place with tweezers. Be sure to leave enough space at the edges for a tight seal. Carefully peel and position second strip. If you get off the track, you may have to do some trimming (another reason to leave a decent margin). Poke a hole in top and loop string through.

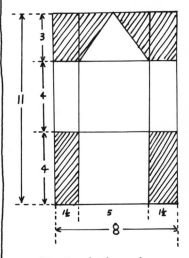

Directions for the envelope

# 9
# Salt Dough Ornaments

Just a sampling of easy-to-make salt dough ornaments

Have you ever worked with salt dough? It's one of the nicest, most well-behaved, most ladylike goops going. It looks nice (pure sugary-white); it feels nice (soft, smooth, not sticky); and it even smells okay. To think that all this is yours for only a quarter! That's about what you pay for the humble ingredients: one cup of table salt and a half-cup of cornstarch. (There are dozens of recipes for salt dough, but this one is the simplest, and it works, so why clutter up our brains?)

The beauty of salt dough, of course, is that it *looks* expensive. In no time at all, and with one hand behind your back, you can turn out ornaments that look for all the world like ceramic or jigsawed wood or papier mâché. Or, if you prefer your salt dough pure and simple, as I do, you can leave your ornaments plain white (and they'll *stay* pristine white, won't fade to a

blah beige). You don't have to do another thing to salt dough ornaments, if you don't want to—they'll dry all by themselves in a day or two. But, if you're impatient, you can also pop them into a slow oven (200 degrees) and pop them out again in an hour or two. If you don't like salt dough's natural bisque-like finish, you can give it anything from a high-gloss coat to an almost translucent porcelain-like finish.

Obviously, even your smallest fry can share in the fun, but don't let anybody tell you that salt dough is strictly kid stuff. Use the offbeat originals you'll spot on these pages as a springboard for your own zingy ideas.

## RECIPE FOR SALT DOUGH *

½ cup cornstarch
⅓ cup water
1 cup salt
⅓ cup water

Dissolve cornstarch in ⅓ cup water in bowl. In separate pan, mix 1 cup salt and ⅓ cup water and heat, stirring constantly until mixture comes to a boil. Remove from heat and stir in cornstarch solution. Stir hard until mixture is the consistency of thick mashed potatoes. (If dough refuses to stiffen as, mysteriously, it sometimes does, return pan to low heat briefly and stir.) Turn dough out on board until cool enough to handle and knead until smooth and pliable. (See page 64 for tips on kneading.) Immediately place into plastic bag and seal; it will keep indefinitely even without refrigeration.

## DIRECTIONS FOR SALT DOUGH ORNAMENTS

Salt dough can be modeled like clay or rolled and cut out like cookie dough. You'll probably want to start with cookie cutter ornaments, and why not? What would Christmas be without Santas, bells, angels, and stars? If you leave them plain white, try "decorating" them with the tip of a knife, with glitter, or sequins. Dress up an airy angel with cutouts, paper doily wings, straw hair, and a halo for a hanger. Or simply embed golden corn kernels in another. Trim a sugary-white tree with colorful rolled-dough balls and candy canes, or use silver sequins and pearls. To make a snowflake

* Unlike some salt dough recipes, this one *can* be doubled.

A batch of salt dough costs only 25¢.

A paper doily makes perfect wings for an angel.

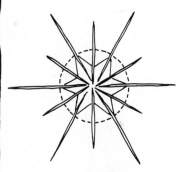

A Scandinavian star made with toothpicks

that's second cousin to expensive Scandinavian straw ones, cut out a 2½-inch circle of dough and embed 12 whole and broken toothpicks as shown. With sharp paring knife, cut out points of star. When dry, coat with clear varnish.

Of course, you can color salt dough, too. Use anything from delicate watercolors (tubes are best) and brilliant acrylics to poster paints and enamels. Paint a holly leaf or wreath in bold ceramic-like hues. Try a few colorful folk art motifs, and add a felt base to your tree. Add white "lace" to a plump red heart and white fur and beard to a jolly Santa. Paint a bell bright turquoise and add sequins and a jeweled clapper. You can also squish food coloring into still-moist dough, but the results are often spotty and the process decidedly messy. Besides, with pre-colored dough, you have to know in advance what you're making and, when it comes to salt dough, who knows what you'll dream up next?

After you tire of cookie cutter ornaments, you'll surely want to try your hand at some "originals." Sculpting with salt dough is literally child's play. You'll think you're back in kindergarten while you roll lumps of dough into mouth-watering apples, oranges, lemons, tomatoes, and pineapples. Decorate them with dough or artificial leaves and use whole cloves for stem ends. For "sugared" strawberries, dip tips in salt (sugar just gets gooey), or dot with white paint.

Speaking of "originals," are you handy with an artist's brush? Paint a miniature ancestor portrait, long-stemmed rose, or landscape, and frame it with gilded squiggles of dough. Believe me, you won't find *these* in any Trim the Tree Shop, or on any other tree on the block. (If Rembrandt you're not, simply cut out a pussycat or floral bouquet or whatever from a magazine and glue it on. Coat with varnish or shellac to preserve it.)

The "night before Christmas" mouse sports pipe cleaner ears and tail, pink snout, and sequin eyes fastened with straight pins. To make a butterfly, roll tubes of dough between your palms and press ends together. Add a macaroni twist for the body and spaghetti bits for antennae. When dry, glue on sheer gift paper or colored cellophane.

Does that bisque-like "Peace" rose look too advanced for you? It's cinchy. Start with a tightly rolled center. Shape balls of dough into thin petals with your fingers and press around center one at a time. (You'll find a helpful drawing on page 88.) Press on dough calyx and leaves. Poke hanging hole through thickest section of rose. Paint to suit.

Salt dough ornaments: the shapes are infinite.

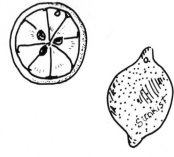

Be sure to make holes for hanging before the dough dries. Hang with clear thread.

Corn kernels trim another angel. *Courtesy of Kay Scarborough.*

Hand-molded mouse has pink sequin eyes.

## TIPS ON WORKING WITH SALT DOUGH

• Don't forget to poke hanging holes in ornaments *before* they dry. Use a metal skewer, needle, or plastic straw.

• Hang ornaments with clear fishing line, embroidery floss, ribbon, gold string, thin wire, or hooked ornament hangers.

• Remove dough only as needed from plastic bag—it dries out fast.

• Add decorations to *moist* dough by simply pressing them on; add decorations to *dry* ornaments with Elmer's glue.

• Remember, salt dough is *heavy*—don't make ornaments too big or too thick.

• Although salt dough may be air-dried or oven-dried, it's quicker to oven-dry thicker pieces.

• For a porcelain-like finish, brush on 2 or 3 coats of one part Elmer's glue to one part water.

• For a high-gloss finish, brush on 2 or 3 coats of clear nail polish, shellac, or varnish. Polyurethane varnish is probably the best. (Aerosol plastic sprays are okay but may require more coats.)

• Store ornaments in sealed plastic bags with mothballs to protect against small wildlife.

• Caution small children that salt dough ornaments are *not* to be eaten. To avoid temptation, don't shape dough into good-enough-to-eat sugar cookies, petit fours, or bonbons.

## MARZIPAN TREATS

While we're at it, why not try your hand at some meant-to-be-eaten marzipan treats?

Beat 2 egg whites until stiff and mix with 1 cup almond paste. Flavor with ½ teaspoon lemon or vanilla extract and add about 1 cup confectioner's sugar, or enough to make the mixture stiff enough to handle. Let stand overnight, covered with a damp cloth. Next day, tint the paste with food colorings and mold into assorted shapes.

A rose is easier than it looks.

Light shines through butterfly's backing.

Use cookie cutters for traditional shapes.

Hand-modeled fruits are fun.

Leave some ornaments pure sugary white.

Framed watercolors

Ornaments may be painted or decorated.

# 10
# Salt Dough Topiary Tree

A colorful topiary tree is made of waxed salt dough fruits.

To me, the most elegant Christmas decoration of all is an 18th-century Williamsburg "apple tree." But I covered that subject in an earlier book. Now, we're not talking about fresh juicy apples, dew-drenched boxwood, and lush leafy pineapples (the ancient symbol of hospitality). We're talking about things that you, not God, can make with your own two hands— out of practically nothing. Here again, the "nothing" is good old salt dough. But this time, instead of painting your fruits, you dip them in colored melted wax. Maybe a salt dough fruit tree isn't quite as toothsome as the real thing, but it will certainly last a lot longer.

Would you like to know what *really* inspired my topiary tree? Bloopers from the preceding ornament operation. What to do with all those plump round oranges and fat-cheeked apples I'd merrily rolled?

Williamsburg "apple tree"

Melt wax in a coffee tin in a pan of water.

Stand waxed fruits in styrofoam to dry.

Secure florist's pinholder to plate with florist's clay.

Obviously, they were much too clunky to hang on a slender Christmas tree bough. That was the beginning of the project—and, to be honest, I thought I'd never see the end. Before you start, let me warn you that topiary trees take a lot more time and a lot more salt dough than a few skinny stars and Santa Clauses. You'll need five or six batches of the recipe given on page 46 for a tree this size. And you can't get started on Christmas Eve.

If all this scares you off, don't go away—you can still play with salt dough fruits. Instead of tackling a time-consuming tree, simply tumble a few bananas, pears, grapes, or what-have-you into a pretty basket. Add a perky plaid bow and a handful of pine cones. Or you can poke your fruits into a wreath, Della Robbia style (be sure to impale them on toothpicks before they harden).

Here's a by-the-by tip for holiday hostesses who'd rather put their sculpting talents to more practical use. Why not make your fruits out of real live cheese? An artist-chef in Pennsylvania sells custom-order cheese creations for very fancy prices, but there's really nothing to it. You can use any semi-soft cheese, such as cheddar or Edam (about 6 to 8 ounces for an apple or pear). Make some halved fruits, too, and paint on pits and veins. Chill modeled fruits in the refrigerator; then finger-paint with *diluted* food coloring. Use whole cloves, twigs, and leaves for extra realism. Arrange on a serving board with fresh greens. (P.S. *You'll* probably have to make the first dent in your too-pretty-to-eat "arrangement.")

## MATERIALS FOR SALT DOUGH TOPIARY TREE

Salt dough (5 to 6 times the recipe on page 46)
Round toothpicks
Household wax (or old candle stubs)
Candle dye (or old crayons)
Whole cloves
Florist's wire
9-inch styrofoam cone
Base for cone
Old, used styrofoam block
Linoleum paste

OPTIONAL

Acrylic paints
Glass compote

52

Florist's clay
Pinholder
Florist's Cling

## DIRECTIONS FOR TOPIARY TREE

Form dough into desired fruit shapes. Press cloves and clove stems into apples, pears, etc. Form strawberry leaves from salt dough (to be painted green later). Spear large fruits with toothpicks. Grapes and cherries are wired into clusters before baking. Bake on cookie sheet for about 8 hours at 200 degrees.

To color fruits, melt wax in coffee tin in pan of water over *low* heat. Always keep an eye on wax on the stove and don't drip any water into it. Add candle dye or crayon bits until you get desired color. Remove wax from water and let cool briefly. Tip can and dip in fruit. Stand in styrofoam block to harden.

For more realistic-looking fruits, touch up with acrylic paints straight from the tube. Or you can add a blush of color to pears and peaches with a smudge of lipstick. Poke "dots" into strawberries and citrus fruits with a hatpin or metal skewer.

Before arranging fruit, secure styrofoam cone firmly to your base. For a permanent decoration, any old, unwanted plate will do, especially if you spray-paint it black or gold. Linoleum paste will hold the cone in place. For a more elegant, temporary base, use a good glass plate. Anchor a florist's pinholder to the plate with florist's clay (form clay into a "snake," press around bottom of holder and then push down on holder with a slightly circular motion). Press cone firmly onto pinholder.

To assemble tree, start with larger fruits at base. Add smaller lemons, limes, and plums as you build. Fill in bare spots with luscious strawberries and tuck fresh greenery around the base, if you like.

To make an instant "compote," secure your plate to an upended goblet with florist's Cling.

Press cone firmly into pinholder.

If a tree is too much trouble, try a casual basket of salt dough fruit.

Use your salt dough sculpting talents to make an intriguing cheese tray.

Wire grapes and cherries into clusters.

# 11
# Tin Can
# Ornaments

Tin can lids make shimmering ornaments and flowers.

At Christmastime, the "tree" on Fisherman's Wharf in Monterey, California, is a shimmery, glimmery sight to see. The local fishmongers drape a huge cone with fishing nets and trim it with hundreds of shiny tin cans—sardine, tuna, shrimp, lobster, crab, mackerel, anchovy, and abalone—that dance in the sunlight and are twice as dazzling by night. Why not add a tinny twinkle to your own Christmas tree? Tin can ornaments are one of the thriftiest tricks I know. Just save the lids from all those cans of juice, soup, fruits, and vegetables that you use every week—you'll collect all that you need in no time. And who knows? Your ornaments may turn into true collector's items some day—there's no telling how long real metal containers will be around.

You can do dozens of fascinating things with tin. Even the simplest star or bell will out-glitter many a

store-bought bauble, but you can add to the glamor by punching out holes, hammering in designs, cutting, fringing, curling, and "etching" your lids. You can turn out birds, fish, and butterflies. You can copy anything from an 18th-century weather vane to Mexican molds to museum-type pre-Columbian amulets. Of course, tin ornaments are a natural for your outdoor tree (although some will rust in time).

If you've never tangled with tin before, it's probably less perilous than you think. I'll admit I started out with my heart in my mouth and heavy gloves on my hands, convinced that the doctor's bills would make this my most expensive project yet. But I was soon snipping merrily away, minus gloves, and I emerged with nary a nick. Just use normal care. Before you find out the hard way, let me clue you that some lids are harder to cut than others and some projects take more patience than others. For a really quick-and-easy out, use disposable aluminum cookie sheets and cupcake holders. Ordinary kitchen shears or even manicure scissors will do the job nicely.

## MATERIALS FOR TIN CAN ORNAMENTS

Tin can lids
Wire cutters or tin snips
Ice pick
Hammer
Beer can opener
Screwdriver
Assorted trims
Fishing line (for hanging)

## DIRECTIONS FOR TIN CAN ORNAMENTS

Wash lids thoroughly, using steel wool or scouring powder to remove price stamps. If one side of lid is dull or mottled, sandwich it against another for a double motif, or spray it gold or silver. (Many silver lids are backed with "gold"—look for them.) To sandwich lids together, use Elmer's glue, or simply line up both hanging holes precisely before stringing. If you don't own an ice pick, use a pointed nail to make hanging holes and to "etch" designs (or metal skewer for very thin metals). Any of these tools, plus a screwdriver or chisel, can be used for hammered designs. Protect your work surface with an old cutting board or block of wood.

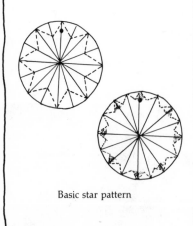

Basic star pattern

## STARS

Make paper tracing of lid and fold paper pattern 4 times, which will give you 16 sections. Tape onto lid (pattern may also be glued on and soaked off later). Cut 8 or 16 points as shown, making cuts as deep as you like. For added shimmer, gently bend every other section slightly forwards.

## SUNBURST

Using basic star pattern, cut 16 very deep points into center. Bend some backwards, some forwards.

## FRINGED FLOWER

Make slanted cuts around border of lid. Bend alternating petals forwards and backwards.

## MEXICAN STAR

This design was adapted from a Mexican tin mold. For center, make paper tracing of 2½-inch lid; fold in half, then thirds, to make 6 sections. Hammer straight lines with screwdriver; etch leaf design with ice pick. For star, make paper pattern of 4-inch lid and again fold into sixths. Cut out points and bend backward. Line up lids; poke matching hanging holes and string together.

## HAMMERED DISK

*Before* removing lid from can, poke openings around edge with beer can opener. Decorate center by pounding with Phillips screwdriver and hammer. Fringe edges.

## MONOGRAMMED DISK

Pencil in name and date for guideline and etch with ice pick. Glue on border of strung silver sequins, or use narrow press-on silver braid. Make one for each member of the family.

## 18TH-CENTURY ANGEL

This airy horn-blowing angel was copied from an antique weather vane. Trace outline and transfer to disposable aluminum cookie sheet by going over lines with sharp pencil or ball point pen. Cut with ordinary scissors.

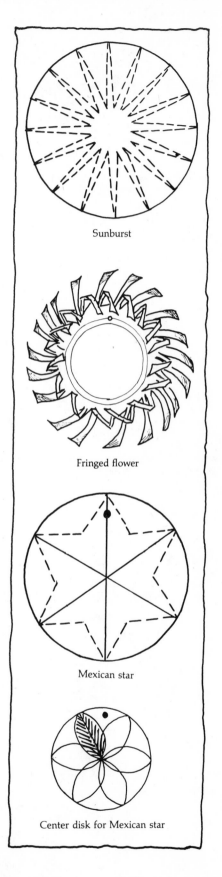

Sunburst

Fringed flower

Mexican star

Center disk for Mexican star

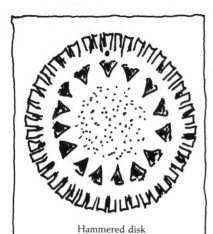

Hammered disk

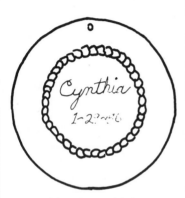

Monogrammed disk

Inca amulet

## INCA AMULET

This is an adaptation of a museum reproduction in brass. The features are formed by pounding on the handles of a screwdriver or ice pick with a hammer.

## BELL

String and knot 3 graduated disks on gold cord. Trim off ragged edges and use trimmings for clapper (or extra icicles on the tree).

## BIRD

Trace and cut out bird pattern. Tape to gold side of 3-inch lid while cutting. For wings, cut another gold lid in half and make slit to attach to body. Glue on sequin eye and feathery tail.

## BUTTERFLY

Trace and transfer body pattern and 2 wing patterns to aluminum cookie sheet. Cut and fold as shown. Staple wings to body and pull "antennae" up. Decorate with felt-tip markers (Speedie brand markers work best on metal).

## FISH

Trace pattern for large fish and tape to 4-inch lid; cut. Cut smaller fish from another lid. Fringe tails; add sequin eyes. String and knot all three together.

## PINWHEEL

Cut 4-inch square from aluminum cookie sheet. Cut diagonal lines as shown from each corner to 1-inch of center. Bring points of each corner to exact center and secure with long gold-headed pin.

## FLOWER HOLDER

Hide bottom stains on anchovy tin with silver spray and glitter. Glue on tiny starflower bouquet and velvet bow.

## TIN CAN FLOWERS

I'm sure you've seen elegant metal flower "sculptures" selling in gift shops for $50 and up. Why not pot up

18th-century angel

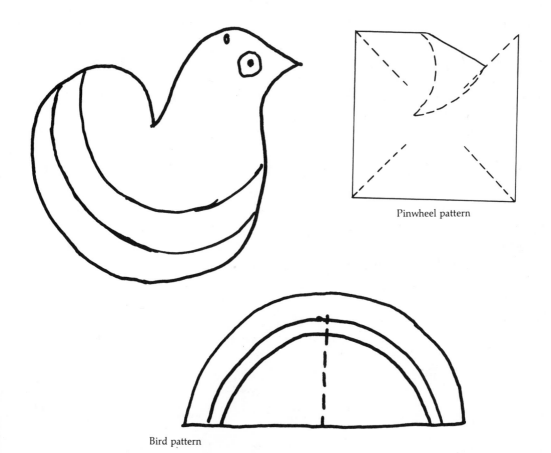

Pinwheel pattern

Bird pattern

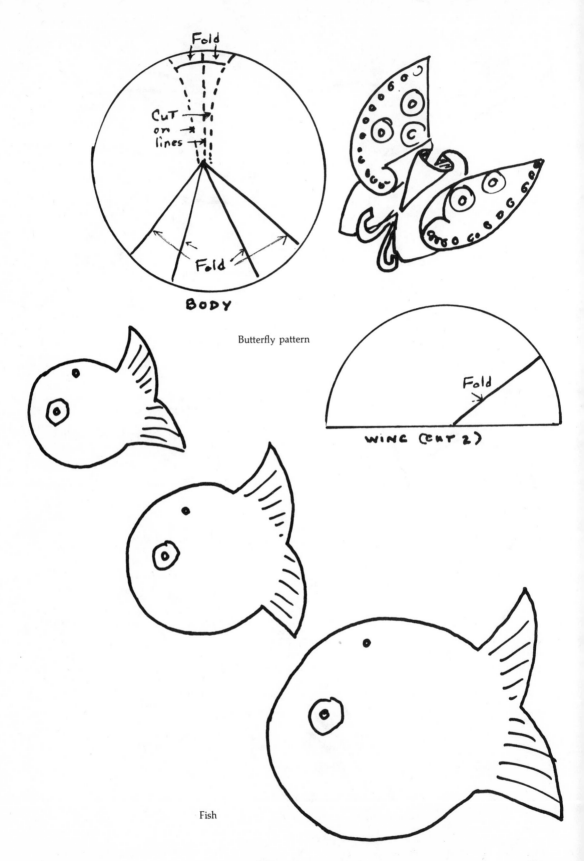

Fold

Cut
on
lines

Fold

BODY

Butterfly pattern

Fold

WING (CUT 2)

Fish

60

your own bouquet of floral dazzlers? For starters, add a
stem to the fringed flower ornament on page 57—then
let your imagination and your tin snips fly. Actually,
I'd suggest limiting your bouquet to maybe two or
three varieties, or, in the case of that out-sized
scouring pad "sunflower," just two or three of a kind.
I've lumped them all together here just to show you
how many different kinds of flowers you can pull out
of a tin can or throwaway cupcake tin.

To wire flowers to stems, poke two holes in lid;
insert wire and twist tightly. (Braided gold wire sold in
crafts shops looks best.) Tape flower to heavy florist's
wire (#16) with florist's tape. The trick is to get a
good tight start at the top, then twirl tape with your
right hand while your left hand pulls down hard.

Weight your container (it could be a shiny tin
can) with sand or stones. Add styrofoam cut to fit;
insert flower stems. You can spray the styrofoam gold
or silver, or camouflage it with more stones.

1. Fringe disposable aluminum cupcake tin. Poke two
   holes in center and wire on metallic mesh scouring
   pad.
2. Cut narrow, slanted fringe around edge of lid;
   pound dots in center.
3. Fringe lid just to center ring; wire on gold lid
   center.
4. Fringe outer edge of lid and twist into curls with
   eyebrow tweezers (fair warning: this takes
   patience).
5. Make a basic paper pattern for a star. Instead of
   cutting points, round off each section. Make large
   8-petal silver flower and smaller 8-petal gold
   flower. Wire a white-tipped pine cone and fasten
   all three together.
6. Using basic pattern for star, make 16 deep cuts
   almost to center. Cut ½-inch-deep V's into each
   section. Bend alternating sections forward. Wire on
   silver sprayed and glittered sweet gum ball.
7. Fringe lid almost to center; bend alternating strips
   or sections forward and backward.

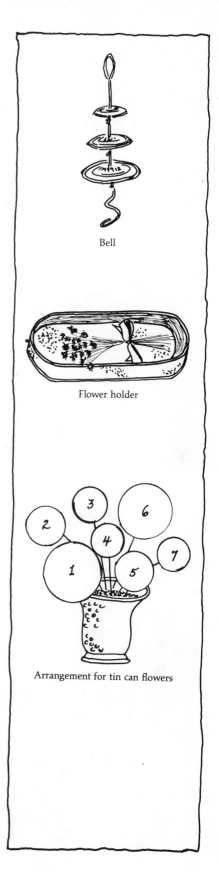

Bell

Flower holder

Arrangement for tin can flowers

# 12
# Braided Bread
# Dough Wreath

Mouth-watering bread dough wreath—to eat or preserve for years

Does this crusty, crunchy, golden-brown wreath look good enough to eat? It is. Or *was,* before it was preserved for posterity with coats of glossy varnish. In fact, when you make this wreath, you'd better plan on making two—one to look at and one to munch on— especially if this is your maiden effort at bread-making. When you pull your first gorgeous, galumptious, glory-be masterpiece out of the oven and get a whiff of the heavenly, ineffable aroma of fresh-baked bread, you'll simply *have* to dig in. You'll scarcely be able to wait till it cools, much less be strong enough to embalm it in shellac.

Incidentally, when it comes time to varnish your second effort, you may feel slightly guilty about wasting all that wholesome goodness, especially in light of the world's food shortage. Would it cheer you up to know that Bergdorf Goodman in New York had one in their window last Christmas priced at $28? It was much smaller, and I estimate the cost of yours at about $1.25. (Minus the "flowers"—dried apricots are out of sight these days.)

If you've never baked a loaf of bread in your life, as I hadn't, let me hasten to assure you that it's not the big mystical deal that everybody seems to think it is. It's a piece of cake. But, if you're still jittery, try to forget that you're b-b-baking b-b-bread. Pretend you're just fooling with another batch of crafts-y glop that's going to wind up on the wall, anyway, not in somebody's stomach, so what's to worry? Why should you care if it's too heavy, too dry, too soggy, too coarse, too streaky, too doughy, or any of the other perils that make ordinary bread-bakers tremble?

True, there are a few hallowed rules for successful bread-making that you'd be foolish to ignore, such as kneading your dough thoroughly and keeping it warm and cozy while it rises. But have a good time. Don't fret if you don't have the proper thermometer to measure your water temperature *exactly.* Don't stew because the recipe nonchalantly calls for "5 to 6 cups" of flour—even old pro's have to play it by ear, because the correct amount varies with each brand of flour. And I hope you wouldn't dream of using one of those newfangled electric bread-kneading attachments. Kneading is half the fun. If you can't spare ten minutes for a little old-fashioned, mother-earthy, tension-releasing pummeling, you might as well buy yourself a plastic dime-store wreath, right?

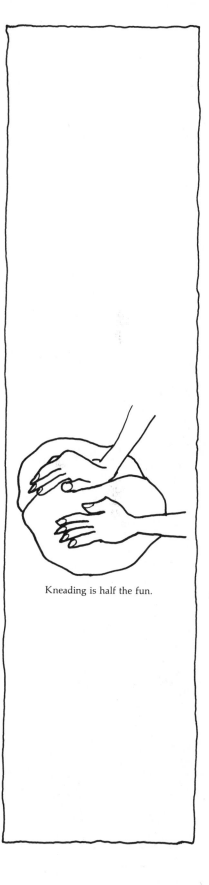

Kneading is half the fun.

Let dough rise in the top of an unheated oven with a pan of boiling water in the bottom.

Braid the dough into a 32-inch rope.

# INGREDIENTS FOR BRAIDED BREAD DOUGH WREATH

½ cup milk
2 tablespoons sugar
2 teaspoons salt
3 tablespoons butter or margarine
1½ cups warm water (105 to 115 degrees F.)
1 package active dry yeast
5 to 6 cups unsifted all-purpose flour
1 egg, beaten
1 tablespoon milk

# DIRECTIONS FOR BRAIDED BREAD DOUGH WREATH

## TO MAKE DOUGH

In saucepan, heat ½ cup milk, the sugar, salt, and butter until warm (120 to 130 degrees F.); cool to lukewarm and set aside. Measure warm water into large warm bowl. Sprinkle in yeast; stir until dissolved. Add milk mixture and 3 cups flour; beat until smooth. With wooden spoon, stir in enough additional flour (about 2 cups) to make a stiff dough. Turn onto lightly floured surface; knead until smooth, satiny, and elastic—about 8 to 10 minutes. (The kneading motion consists of folding the dough back on itself, again and again, while pushing it lightly and rhythmically with the palms of your hands.) Place dough in greased bowl, turning to grease top of dough. Cover with tea towel; let rise in warm place, free from drafts, until doubled in bulk, about 1 hour. (One of the best warm, cozy places for your bowl is the top shelf of your unheated oven, with a pan of boiling water set on the lowest shelf.)

## TO FORM WREATH

Punch dough down. Punching down consists of plunging the hand down into the dough until it is flattened; the edges are then folded in toward the center and the dough turned over so that the smooth side is on the top. (This breaks the large gas pockets and helps develop an even grain.) Divide dough into 3 equal pieces. On lightly floured surface, roll or shape each dough piece into a 32-inch rope. Join all three at one end by pressing together; interlace them to form a braid. On a greased baking sheet, shape braid into a ring about 10 inches in diameter. Seal ends together.

Cover; let rise in warm place, free from drafts, until almost doubled in bulk, about 30 minutes.

## TO BAKE WREATH

Combine egg and 1 tablespoon milk; brush mixture gently on wreath. Bake in preheated oven at 400 degrees for about 35 minutes or until golden brown. Bread is done if it sounds hollow when tapped lightly. For higher glaze, brush wreath twice during baking. Cover with foil, if necessary, to prevent uneven browning. Remove from baking sheet and cool on rack.

## TO DECORATE WREATH

Use dried apricots for "petals" of flowers. Secure with round toothpicks broken in half. Center with whole dried apricot and red gumdrop on toothpick. Stick leaf-shaped spearmint candy around flower or tuck green gumdrop "leaves" between the petals. For edible centerpiece, serve warm with softened butter and assorted delicious preserves.

## TO PRESERVE WREATH

Brush with two or three light coats of shellac or varnish. Let dry thoroughly. Trim with gay ribbon bow and hang from window, wall, or kitchen door with clear fishing line. This is one Christmas wreath you don't have to take down but, if you do, store it in a sealed plastic bag with a smattering of moth balls. (I'd recommend giving the wreath one overall coat of shellac before adding your decorations, for extra protection.) Bread dough wreaths, either edible or eternal, make marvelous gifts, and it's a nice gesture to include the recipe with your offering.

## ANOTHER HOME-BAKED BREAD IDEA

Bake bread in loaf shape (follow recipe in any cookbook); shellac or varnish. Tie with gingham ribbon and mount on breadboard trimmed with matching glued-on gingham. Many bread dough "sculptures" such as this are currently popular in the better handcrafts boutiques. And, if you're really lazy or strapped for time, why not shellac your stale, dry store-bought breads, rolls, or pretzels for posterity?

Make flowers from dried apricots and gum drops.

Bread dough sculpture also makes a "delicious" present.

# 13
# Heirloom
# Ornaments

Handmade heirloom ornaments

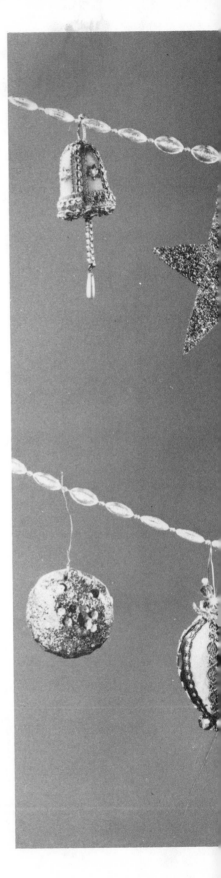

We used to trim our tree in "neon roadhouse" style, just like everybody else, with hundreds of shiny balls, dozens of multicolored lights, and tons of tinsel. In fact, thanks to my Lord & Taylor husband, our tree usually out-glittered, out-gaudied, and out-weighed all the others on the block. But things are different now. It began with a handful of extra-special one-of-a-kind imported ornaments. Then the kids went off to kindergarten and we had still more precious hand-mades to hang. Eventually, I got into the act, of course—why should *they* have all the fun? By now, our little hoard of special ornaments has grown so fat that we trim our tree with nothing but "heirlooms." There's no room for anything else.

Making your own ornaments is much more exciting than buying them, not to mention cheaper. You know what "fancy" ornaments go for these days. Even if you add only one or two treasures each year, you'll be surprised at how fast they'll pile up—and at

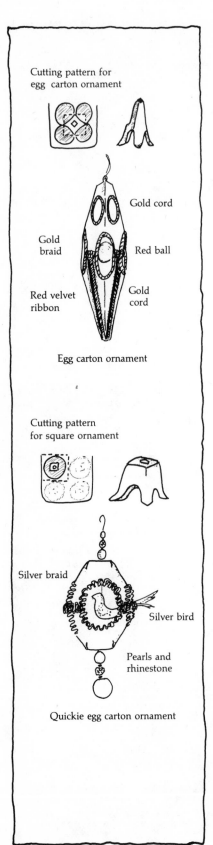

Cutting pattern for
egg carton ornament

Gold cord

Gold
braid

Red ball

Red velvet
ribbon

Gold
cord

Egg carton ornament

Cutting pattern
for square ornament

Silver braid

Silver bird

Pearls and
rhinestone

Quickie egg carton ornament

how merry the tree-trimming task can be. Even taking *down* the tree is less grisly when you know each dear little bibelot by heart.

## RIBBON AND BEAD ORNAMENTS

Of course, there are those kits you can buy, with all the trimmings you need neatly packaged inside. But who wants ornaments that look like everybody else's? Besides, you can gather trimmings that are twice as elegant for half the cost. The best place to look for ribbon is the sewing department of a big department store, or a large fabric shop. They usually have the best selection of velvets, satins, florals, plaids, and other pretties in a complete range of colors—as well as lace edgings, braids, and other trims. (Don't try to save yourself some work by buying wide ribbon—it's a pain in the neck to pin onto a round ball. The narrower the ribbon, the better.) Don't settle for ordinary Christmasy red and green—look for off-beat colors for your very own custom-designed creations. Use hot orange, pale pink, peacock blue, deep burgundy, even chocolate brown (you may luck into bargains at the remnant counter).

For trims, your best bet is your own jewelry drawer. You're bound to have broken beads, mateless earrings, cast-off brooches, and some hideous gift jewelry that you've never even taken out of the box. Break it up and put it to good use. Next, try the thrift shops. For nickels and dimes, you can buy strings of pearls and other razzle-dazzle necklaces that will net you whole boxes full of glittering bead trims. Hobby shops and specialty stores like The Christmas Shop in Williamsburg, Virginia, sell all kinds of loose "jewels," paillettes, sequins, and fascinating tops and bottoms for your ornaments, also for nickels and dimes. (To keep cut strings of beads or sequins from unraveling, stick a piece of Scotch tape at the ends.)

Now, all you need is a supply of styrofoam balls and a slew of straight pins. Unfortunately, the teardrop, bell, and other fancy styrofoam shapes you see here aren't sold in every crafts shop, but keep your eyes open, wherever you wander. On the other hand, don't overlook the unusual bases you have lying right around the house, such as wooden spools and, to be sure, toilet paper rolls. (Glue trims onto spools; use glue or pins for cardboard rolls.)

I won't insult your IQ with step-by-step directions for the beribboned and bejewelled ornaments pictured. The sketched designs are self-explanatory, and you'll

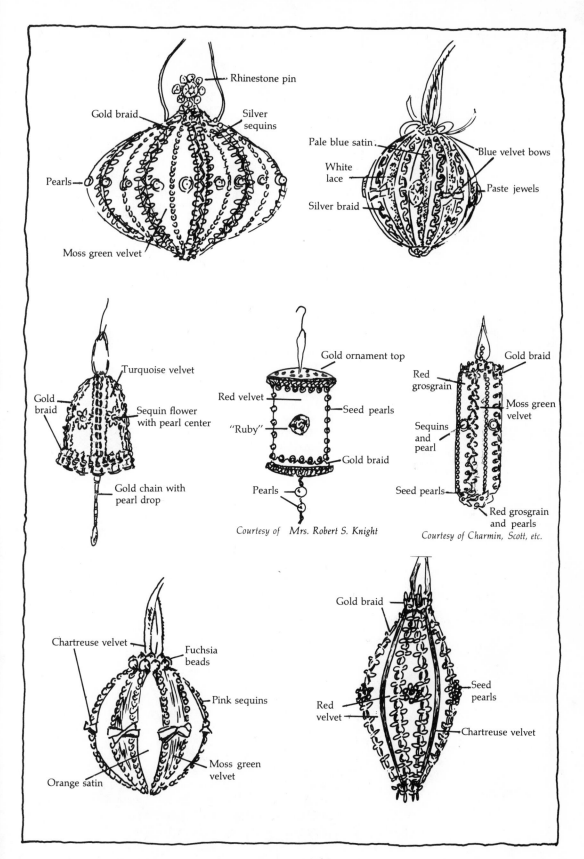

Rhinestone pin

Gold braid

Silver sequins

Pearls

Moss green velvet

Pale blue satin

White lace

Silver braid

Blue velvet bows

Paste jewels

Turquoise velvet

Gold braid

Sequin flower with pearl center

Gold chain with pearl drop

Gold ornament top

Red velvet

"Ruby"

Seed pearls

Gold braid

Pearls

*Courtesy of Mrs. Robert S. Knight*

Gold braid

Red grosgrain

Moss green velvet

Sequins and pearl

Seed pearls

Red grosgrain and pearls

*Courtesy of Charmin, Scott, etc.*

Chartreuse velvet

Fuchsia beads

Pink sequins

Moss green velvet

Orange satin

Gold braid

Red velvet

Seed pearls

Chartreuse velvet

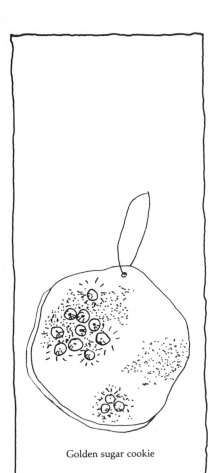

Golden sugar cookie

probably want to try your own anyway. I note the various trims just to get you out of your color rut. Directions for the other heirloom ornaments follow.

## PAPIER-MÂCHÉ BIRD

Trace bird shape and cut out of heavy cardboard. Tear newspaper into thin strips; dip in wheat paste and wind around and around form until desired thickness. Dry completely. Paint bird solid color; add decoration; spray with clear plastic. Poke hole for hanging. *Courtesy of Cynthia Lamb O'Neill at age 10.*

## GOLDEN SUGAR COOKIE

Draw circle on heavy cardboard and papier mâché as above. For fatter cookie, pad with newspaper or paper toweling. Dry. Add gold spray, glitter, and sequins.

## EGG CARTON ORNAMENTS

A. Remove 2 high-peaked dividers from egg carton by cutting in square around the peak with small, sharp scissors. Cut "windows" in top section. Paint inside of each section black. Punch hole in top section; insert small Christmas ball on gold cord and knot it with loop for hanging. Glue sections together and coat with gesso. When dry, paint gold with brush. Antique by rubbing on diluted black oil paint and wiping off with cheesecloth. Glue on red velvet ribbon, gold cord, and gold braid. *Courtesy of Mrs. Robert S. (Peg) Knight.*

B. Here's a quickie version of Mrs. Knight's ornament, in case you don't have gesso, et cetera. Remove 2 sections from short cup egg carton by cutting in square around the cup. Enlarge the openings; staple or glue together. Spray with 2 coats of silver paint. Trim with self-stick silver braid, silver bird, and thrift shop jewels strung on wire. Or use your bright pastel egg carton as is, with a coat of plastic spray for longer life.

## GOLD STAR SPANGLE

Trace star and tape paper pattern to copper screening while cutting out. Spray gold or coat with Elmer's glue and thick layer of gold glitter. *Courtesy of Mrs. William A. (Audrey) Patterson.*

Pattern for papier-mâché bird

Pattern for star

71

# 14
# Nature
# Ornaments

Nothing makes an artsy-craftsy happier than finding another make-it-yourself nut on the block. Lucky me, I have not only one but several extra-special friends and neighbors who like to do things with their hands. A few years ago, we fell casually into the habit of exchanging handmade ornaments with each other each Christmas. It's a delightsome custom and one of the

Nature ornaments from simple outdoor gatherings

Velvet Saint Nick

"Make-it-Merry" presents and decorations for Christmas

Heirloom ornaments

surprise-package joys of the season that I look forward to most. Many of the trinkets on these pages were born that way.

One of the ground rules, of course, is that our little doodads cost no money. When you're trying to come up with something new and different and *cheap*, there's nothing like good old Mother Nature. Look around you with a garden clubber's "seeing eye" and you'll find more precious, priceless materials for ornaments than the fanciest hobby-and-crafts head-quarters could supply. There are nuts and cones, pods and corn husks, seashells and birds' nests, and, by all means, your own home-dried flowers. If you haven't yet tumbled to the great penny-pinching trick of flower drying, believe me, it's so simple a two-year-old can do it. (You'll find the basics on page 35.)

To me, these natural, born-free ornaments are some of the most elegant treasures on the tree. Even a lowly wishbone can turn into a thing of beauty (in our house, we save the Thanksgiving turkey wishbone each year to gussy up for a special aunt—to make an annual New Year's Eve wish on).

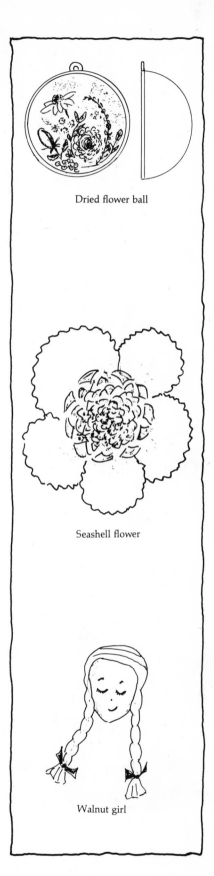

Dried flower ball

Seashell flower

Walnut girl

## DRIED FLOWER BALLS

Press small wad of Stickum to one half of a take-apart clear plastic ball (see Glossary). Carefully insert dried flowers and leaves; close ball. It's a nice idea to identify the flowers in a gift ball. Here you'll see zinnias, black-eyed Susans, ageratum, baby's breath, Lemon Drop marigolds, verbena, love-in-a-mist, blue salvia, statice, delphinium, and daffodils (yes, you can dry even daffodils—in silica gel in the oven). Can you think of a more exquisite 50¢ gift?

## SEASHELL FLOWER

Dip tips of five scallop shells in Elmer's glue and insert in scales of pine cone. Twist wire around cone to hang. Dust lightly with gold spray and glitter.

## WALNUT PEOPLE

Bake walnuts to prevent bugs. Drill hole for hanging; spray with gold paint. Paint on face with black felt-tip pen and decorate with sequin eyes, yarn hair, etc. For gifts, personalize each nut with curly red hair, long brown tresses, or blond pigtails, as the case may be. (For small-fry nieces and nephews, split and hollow out the nuts and tuck a crisp folded bill inside—"crack me open, please!" Glue halves back together.)

Oyster shell

Milkweed pods

Glorified wishbone

Bird's nest

## OYSTER SHELL

Clean shell thoroughly. Drill hanging hole with electric drill; gild. Glue on snowy "angel hair" and tiny gold angel, or any other miniature figure. *Courtesy of Mrs. Robert S. (Peg) Knight.*

## MILKWEED PODS

Gather pods in fall; remove silk and hang to dry. (Milkweed grows wild almost everywhere.) Separate "petals" and decorate with everything from other wildlings and a tiny bird on shiny red lacquer to a miniature deer on white satin with silver braid and glitter. Pierce hanging holes with a pin. *Courtesy of Mrs. Charles L. (Joyce) Hayes and Mrs. William A. (Liz) Hubbard.*

## CORN HUSK ANGELS

See page 78 for preparation of corn husks. Gather 2 or 3 damp husks at least 5 inches long in the middle and tie with string. To form head, pull husks down as though you were peeling a banana; tie about 1 inch down with string. For wings, round off ends of 2 more husks; fasten at neck with narrow strip of husk. Fan out shucks and pin to styrofoam block or weight with heavy object until dry. Add face, halo, and hair (corn silk, tinsel, yarn, or thread) if desired, but authentic corn husk dolls are seldom decorated. If your husks are too short, you can cover a 1-inch foam ball or wad of paper toweling and then attach body and wings at the neck.

## GLORIFIED WISHBONE

Thoroughly clean and dry your Thanksgiving turkey wishbone. Spray gold and decorate with glitter, sequins, red starflowers, and narrow orange velvet kiss-me-bows. Obviously, this is just one start-you-off possibility—try using pretty little seashells, pearls, and other dazzling jewels.

## BIRD'S NEST

Real birds' nests are the best. I found my favorite deep in Maryland's rolling hunt country—it's made of pure black horsehair and, though Christmasy it's not, I wouldn't gild it for a sure tip on the Preakness. Nests are easy to spot after the leaves have fallen, but be absolutely sure yours has been deserted. Nests on the ground are the safest bets. Spray thoroughly with insecticide. Or you can build your own in seconds out of excelsior, straw, or even Easter basket hay mixed with thin wheat paste. For eggs, use pebbles, jelly beans, peas, beans, etc. Hang nest from three strings to prevent tipping; or glue it to a clip-on clothespin. Tuck in a copy of the old legend:

> The best of life will come to thee
> If a bird nests in your Christmas tree.

*Courtesy of Mrs. G. Curtis (Kay) Scarborough and John.*

## GILDED SEASHELLS

What nicer way to display those vacation gatherings tucked away in the basement? Spray lightly with gold and/or silver; decorate with glitter, sequins, pearls, or a "diamond." If you think they're too pretty to "lose" in the big tree, give them a place of honor in the greens festooning your mantel. *Courtesy of Cynthia Lamb O'Neill.*

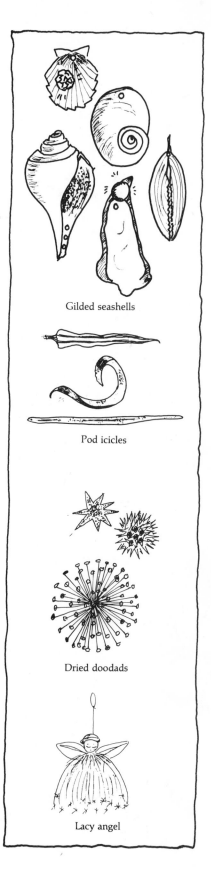

Gilded seashells

## POD ICICLES

Here are some more real "quickies" for the tree. How long can it take to spray-and-glitter natural tree or plant pods to turn them into twinkly, shimmery icicles? And don't think these pods are rare, exotic specimens. Catalpa and honey locust trees grow almost everywhere—just look on the ground (or up in the air). The okra I grow especially for its pods (with a few token harvestings for my husband, the reigning soup king of the neighborhood).

Pod icicles

## DRIED DOODADS

The star is a sliced teasel calyx (no two are alike) with gold spray and multicolor glitter. The spiky ball is a sweet gum pod with silver spray and glitter. The snowflake is 2 giant allium heads glued together, sprayed gold, and dipped in multicolor glitter. *Courtesy of Mrs. William A. (Audrey) Patterson.*

Dried doodads

## LACY ANGEL

Drill hole in acorn for head and insert 3 to 4 inches of wire. Twist at top for hanging and cover bottom end with florist's tape. Wire on 2 swamp milkweed pods for wings. Wire on "bird's nest" seed pod of Queen Anne's lace for skirt. Spray gold. (Hickory oak acorns have marvelous curly-top "wigs.") *Courtesy of Mrs. Thomas C. (Harriet) Flotte.*

Lacy angel

# 15
# Nature
# Flowers

Nature flowers made of corn husks and other surprises

Have you ever tried to coax last year's Christmas poinsettias into bloom again? It can be done. But it's such a pain that I'd rather go out and buy new ones, or, better still, make my own "natural fakes" that will last year after year without coddling. Poinsettias made from milkweed pods are an old, old garden club trick, but you don't have to stick to the same old gaudy red ones. Try some ethereal white ones, too, or the dazzling new pink varieties. In fact, there's nothing wrong with leaving them *au naturel.*

You'll probably use your poinsettias mostly for Christmas decorations, but there are dozens of other flowers you can concoct from natural materials to enjoy year round. And can you think of a niftier gift for your flower-loving friends? Never mind all those low-brow, high-dollar artificial flowers in the stores—there's not a one can compare with a simple, fresh-from-the-farm corn husk peony. Or how about a bevy of corn husk dogwood blossoms (wired to a real

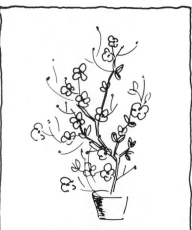

Color tips of dogwood blossoms with red Magic Marker; use black-eyed Susan seed pods for centers.

CORNHUSK WILD-FLOWERS

$1.20 a stem

Corn husk flowers are rare in stores, and outrageously expensive.

Poinsettia made from milkweed pods

dogwood branch) to bring spring into the house all winter long? Corn husk flowers are not only elegant-looking, long-lasting, dirt-cheap, easy-to-make, and as just-like-real as you care to make them, but they also "go" with every decor imaginable. No need to guess whether a faraway aunt or friend goes in for far-out wall graphics or four-poster beds. Best of all, corn husk flowers are still blissfully rare and exclusive. The only ones I've seen for sale were advertised by an obscure Washington, D.C., shop—for $1.20 a stem!

The designs here are my own fumbling first-trys, and I'm sure you can come up with bigger and better ideas. The methods, too, are my own—chances are even your school kids could show you an easier way. (P.S. I'll give specific directions for only the trickier flowers.)

Once in love with corn husks, you'll see flowery possibilities all around you. Why *not* poke dried magnolia leaves into a pine cone for a giant-sized daisy? Just one planted in a clear Lucite pot would be eye-popping in a contemporary room. Paint your daisy white and yellow, if you like, but natural beige is much classier. For your more traditional friends, cluster glycerinized galax leaves into a velvety, chocolate-brown "rose."

## DIRECTIONS FOR MILKWEED POD POINSETTIA

Poke a tiny hole in the fat end of 5 or 6 opened milkweed pods (preferably with center divider intact). Wire each pod individually and twist together into a rosette. Spray with red, gold, or other paint. (I touched my flowers up with artist's acrylics, but it really isn't necessary.) Wire or glue on sweet gum ball for center. Attach flower to heavier wire stem with florist's tape. Tuck your poinsettias into a silver bowl of fresh greens or pin them to a wreath.

## DIRECTIONS FOR CORN HUSK FLOWERS

You *can* buy already prepared corn husks (see Glossary of Materials), but isn't that cheating? Instead, save the best-looking husks from your next corn-on-the-cob feast. Cut off the pointy end and lower binding section from each. Soak overnight in Clorox and water (about ⅓ cup to 1 gallon of water) to bleach. Rinse; squeeze out excess water; press to dry between layers of newspaper under a rug or absorbent toweling in telephone book for one week or less. Fully dried husks can be resoaked or moistened under the tap for greater pliability. *Barely damp* husks work best, but husks must be dried first. (P.S. You can play it both ways by gathering already dried husks in the fall at your nearest friendly farm.)

For leaves, you can use the coarse dark-green outer shucks. Simply cut them with scissors or pinking shears. Husks can also be painted green (or dyed, if you're making lots of leaves or want to try different colored flowers).

## PEONY

With scissors, round off fat ends of 8 to 10 dampened husks about 5 inches long. Fringe lightly by hand. Gather half of the petals at the base and wire with thin florist's wire. Add remaining petals; spread out and fluff. Wire yellow-painted sweet gum ball to heavy wire stem and insert through center. Trim off excess husk ends; wrap stem with florist's tape, using twists of tape for calyx at base of flower. Tape on leaf shapes if desired. When flower dries, it will resemble the famous single-type peony called "Krinkled White" (a great choice for your garden, by the way).

## CHRYSANTHEMUMS

For curly football mum, dampen 10 to 12 of your fattest husks, about 5 to 6 inches long. Roll around stick; tie with twistems; and dry in 250-degree oven for about 15 minutes. Unroll husks carefully one at a time and weight the narrow, still-damp end with a brick; shred husk about ¾ of the way down. Cluster curled sections together to make flower, wiring as you go. Add stem, calyx, and pinked leaves, as before.

For shaggy spider mum, loop over 6 narrow damp strips and twist together with wire. This is flower center. Fill out flower with narrow 8-inch-long strips gathered in the middle. (Wire about 6 to 12 strips at a time and attach until flower is desired size.) Curl some strips around your fingers. Add stem, calyx, and leaves as before.

## DIRECTIONS FOR MAGNOLIA LEAF DAISY

You're probably familiar with deep-brown glycerinized magnolia leaves, but did you know that magnolia dries

For leaves, use coarse, dark-green outer shucks.

Corn husk peony

Magnolia leaf daisy

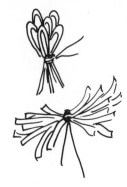

Wrap husks around a stick and tie with twistems for curly mum.

Weight with a brick while shredding into curls.

For shaggy mum, wire looped strips for center; add layers of petals.

Magnolia leaf branch

Round off magnolia leaves and poke into cone.

Ginkgo leaf

Start galax leaf "rose" with a tightly rolled center.

Galax leaf

a luscious, satiny honey-blond color without any treatment at all? Just lay a few fresh branches in an out-of-the-way corner for a month or two. Swish leaves clean in sudsy warm water and dry. For an even higher gloss, coat with neutral shoe polish or plastic spray. (I left mine "as is" to show you their natural sheen. I also included some spotty and holey leaves to cheer you on.) Trim really bad spots with scissors and round off the pointed tips for a daisy-like petal.

Wire pine cone to heavy wire stem (here it's a golden-tan piñon cone); wrap stem with brown florist's tape. Insert leaves between scales, trimming stem ends or adding Elmer's glue if needed. You can make stem leaves more interesting by holding them over steam and reshaping them (many brittle dried leaves can be made supple again this way).

## DIRECTIONS FOR GALAX LEAF ROSE

In most parts of the country, galax leaves are a florist's item. You may even have to special-order them, but they're not expensive (about 24 leaves for under $1). It takes 8 to 12 leaves to make one rose. To preserve leaves, stand stems in solution of 1 part glycerin to 2 parts water until mixture has reached top of leaf (about 2 weeks). Wipe off excess.

To make rose, roll one leaf into a very tight center and wire. Add petals in overlapping circles, wiring as needed. Use largest leaves for last layer and bend them outward. (You can substitute any round-shaped leaf, such as ginkgo—or even ordinary ivy leaves.)

# 16
# Your-
# Own-Thing
# Candles

Many "your-own-thing" candles are simply molded in sand.

It wouldn't be Christmas without candles. But I hope you wouldn't dream of buying one of those razzle-dazzle creations at frazzle-dazzle prices that stream into the stores at Christmas. If you've never tried making your own candles and think there's some kind of XYZ-mystique about it, you won't believe how ABC-simple it is.

You don't need to read books filled with technical directions or sign up for candlemaking classes. You don't need all those fancy supplies sold in candlemaking shops. And you certainly don't need those $2 molds in the shape of an Oriental goddess or simpering elf. All you need to make the candles you see here are ordinary household wax from the supermarket, a few old crayons, and either a bucket of beach sand or assorted makeshift molds that you already have around the house, plus 69¢ for wicking to make enough candles to light up the whole town.

You'll notice that I've skipped the usual do-it-yourselfs that have already been done to death—milk carton candles, juice can candles, and cracked ice candles. I'll also skip the finer points that can be found in dozens of trusty, one-track-minded candlemaking books. I don't bother with stearic acid, hardening crystals, propane torches, candy thermometers, and other picky-pickies, so why ask you to? And this is one candlemaking shop where you won't have to hold your nose.

To me, candlemaking is one of the most relaxing, soul-satisfying, and self-expressing crafts there is. Not to mention cheap, and *useful,* too. Although that cookie cutter star and tree date back to my children's pre-school days, I've really just begun to dabble in wax. So, I'll pass on my own top-of-the-head ideas and seat-of-the-pants methods—but only to get you started making *your*-own-thing candles in your own crafty ways.

## SAND CANDLES

Sand candles are probably the easiest kind of candle there is. All that's required is the amazing ability to dig a hole in the sand, just as you did when you were two. Now, can you take your finger and poke three more holes in your hole? Even the simplest caveman tripod candle is better-looking than many commercial monstrosities. But that's just the beginning of the fascinating things you can do with sand. Add a hunk of driftwood to your "bowl" (here it's a dried California kelp root, with a sprinkling of white gravel).

Candle wax—right from the supermarket

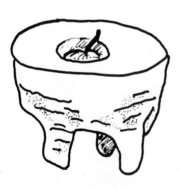

Cookie cutter candles

A simple tripod sand candle

Embed hobby shop "jewels" in the sides, or use glass chips, pretty pebbles, or tiny seashells. The white candle was made with frosty moth crystals.

Dig *three* holes, side by side. Sculpt an oversized free-form shape and, before the wax hardens, scoop out a hole for a water-loving plant such as wandering Jew. Instead of digging a hole, press a favorite seashell or any other shape into the damp sand to form your mold.

Remember that sand should be just damp enough to hold a wall. It should also be uniformly moist and well-packed. Good old free-to-all beach sand is best, because refined commercial sand doesn't cling as well. Remember that the hotter the wax and the drier the sand, the thicker the crust. Your sand candle *can* be dug up in as little as an hour, but it's best to cool it (you and your candle) for 24 hours. You'll find more detailed directions and tips later in the chapter.

## MAKESHIFT MOLDS

Look around you—you have more candle molds than the best-stocked shop, and much more interesting ones. You can use anything you own made of metal or glass—gelatin molds, muffin tins, cookie cutters, tin cans or boxes—everything from ordinary drinking glasses and jelly jars to a fancy bowl.

Or you can leave the candle right in the glass you pour it in. Don't worry, even the most fragile hollow-stemmed champagne glass won't shatter—the trick is to cool the wax slightly and warm the glass beforehand. Talk about recycling—can you think of a better way to use all those chipped and unmatched oldies on their way to the thrift shop or the trash can? Not to mention the cocktail glasses that nobody uses these on-the-rocks days. Fill an unwanted beer mug with amber colored wax and add a "head" of frothy whipped wax. Or shake up a strawberry ice cream soda (easy-does-it on the pink, please).

## SMASHABLE MOLDS

Then there are molds you don't care about shattering. Use any empty, useless bottle, glass, or jar with an interesting shape or texture. Even a prized $75 brandy bottle might better be preserved in wax than languish on a basement shelf. If your container has a narrow neck, use a funnel when pouring. When the candle is done, get out the hammer and have a bang-up coming-

84

out party. Use several double-strength grocery bags and try to stop at the first tinkle. A light crack on the bottom may be all you need, but thick bottles are more stubborn and you don't want to damage the candle.

You can make egg candles in the same way. Cut a ¾-inch hole in the fat end of an egg (where the air pocket is); empty the contents and rinse out. Set in egg carton while pouring wax and, when cool, simply peel off the shell.

## MATERIALS FOR CANDLEMAKING

Paraffin (household wax)
Candle dye, wax crayons, or candle stubs
Wicking
Wick tabs
Beach sand
Makeshift household molds
Coffee tins
Tongs
Funnel
Ice pick
Vegetable oil or silicone spray
Paring knife
Assorted trims

## DIRECTIONS FOR CANDLEMAKING

Melt wax in coffee tin set in small amount of water in larger saucepan. Use very low heat and never leave melting wax unattended. Add candle dye, wax crayons, or candle stubs until you get the color you want. While you're waiting for wax to melt, prepare mold. Coat metal and glass molds with oil or silicone spray for easier release. Prepare wick.

### POSITIONING WICK

Proper wicking is a must for candles—don't try to make do with ordinary string. Wick tabs are a frill, but so inexpensive they're worth it. Simply pull the wick through the tab; close the prongs firmly with pliers; drop tab to bottom of mold after pouring. Or instead of a tab, make a coil in the bottom of the wick and anchor to mold with a drop of melted wax before pouring. For sand candle, simply push wick tab into bottom of hole. It's important that all wicks be centered as exactly as possible (with the naked eye, in

Melt wax in a coffee tin in a saucepan of water over low heat.

Wick tab. Center the wick by tying it to a pencil and centering it, by eye, over the top of the mold.

You can also center the wick with masking tape.

A sand candle with seaweed embellishments

Champagne glass filled with wax is sprinkled with silver sequins.

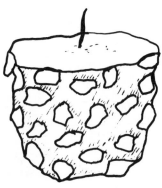

Red sand candle with jewels

Simply press a seashell into sand to form mold.

Add glitter and grapes to a cocktail glass candle.

An ice-cream soda glass is a perfect mold for a youngster's candle.

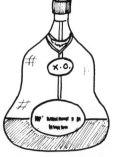

Bottles of any shape make perfect "smashable molds." Use a funnel to pour wax into small-necked bottles.

Eggs are easy "smashable molds."

my book.) To keep wick centered, wind it around a pencil or stick laid across the mold. Or poke it through a slit in masking tape.

But all of this is the *hard* way to add your wick. The easiest way is to add it *after* your candle is made. Poke a straight-down hole into the center with a hot ice-pick; immediately drop in prewaxed wick.

## POURING WAX

Remove can of melted wax from water; set on newspapers to dry bottom so it won't drip into your mold and to cool briefly. Pour into mold or hole in sand. DON'T pour it all; always leave a little dividend in the can for "topping." Topping means filling in the hole that invariably forms as wax cools. Before topping, poke the hole a few times to get rid of any air pockets. Set candle aside to harden. Hardening time will vary with the size and shape of the candle. After unmolding candle, set it aside to "cure" in a cool, not cold, place for at least 24 hours before burning it. Cut wick about ½ to ¾ inch long.

## FINISHING TOUCHES

That's all there is to it. You've just made your first candle! It's probably perfect, just as is, but if not, here's what to do. To remove ragged edges or other flaws, plunge it quickly into boiling water. The experts also use a propane torch to make repairs or create special effects, but you can make do with a lighted taper or match. To make your candle shiny, give it another quickie in-and-out wax dip. For an even glossier sheen, dunk it immediately into cold water. This extra wax dip is especially good for sand candles, to get rid of loose sand.

Don't be afraid to use a knife. You can do lots of repairing, smoothing, shaving, and shaping with an ordinary paring knife. Or you can sculpt, carve designs in, or add texture to your candle with a beer can opener or wooden sculpting tools. Of course, you can also paint your candle, glitter it, or add any other trims you like. But I'd better stop before this chapter gets as long as all the professional candlemaking books.

# DIRECTIONS FOR WATERMELON CANDLE

I saw my first watermelon candle in a snooty decorating studio. Unfortunately, it wasn't for sale, but

Pouring wax. Always reserve a small amount of wax to fill the hole left after the candle sets.

Make a watermelon candle in a gelatin mold.

A watermelon candle comes out green, pink, and white with three separate pours.

A rose candle: Form petals with your fingers and roll tightly for the center. Cut leaves with pinking shears.

A finished rose candle on a thrift-shop saucer

Test colors in small jiggers. They also make beautiful, marble-like mini-candles.

I thought of it the next time I made Jell-O. (Actually, watermelon rinds *aren't* ribbed, so any oval mold will do. Or sculpt your melon in the sand.) It took some head-scratching, but here's the trick I hit on—just keep pouring and digging out.

Coat copper gelatin mold with vegetable oil. Fill with dark green wax (about ½ pound for a 6-inch mold). As soon as the outer rim hardens, in 10 to 15 minutes, spoon out the soft wax in the middle. Fill mold with white wax; let harden till white band is twice as wide as green. Scoop out middle as before. Fill with watermelon-pink wax and add dried watermelon seeds. (If melon is not in season, substitute beans or sunflower seeds.) Scratch in some white veins. If candle is stubborn and difficult to unmold, dip in hot water just like Jell-O. Insert wick in finished candle, using the hot ice-pick method.

## DIRECTIONS FOR ROSE CANDLE

I discovered "soft wax" accidentally, when the phone rang right in the middle of a watermelon candle. Before I knew it, I'd "doodled" all my green scoopings-out into something resembling leaves. So why not turn the pink glop into a rose? Luckily for you and me, I've since found a more sensible way to make flower candles.

Pour melted wax onto a cookie sheet lined with wax paper; pull off thin pieces, one at a time, to form into petals. Use your fingers to thin out and curl the edges. To make rose, start with a tightly rolled center and press on each new petal as you make it. Sheet wax hardens fast; you may have to remelt and repour it. Or try slipping it into a low-low oven (another advantage of the cookie sheet). Mixing beeswax (about one third) with your paraffin will keep it pliable, too, but beeswax is expensive.

Cut around edges of leaves with pinking shears and make veins with your fingernails. Press fine florist's wire into leaves while they are still soft to curve them; the wire can then be pressed into rose. Dip finished flower in cold water. Arrange cooled flowers on a 5¢ thrift shop plate; anchor them with dribbles of melted wax.

## TIPS ON CANDLEMAKING

• Never pour wax down the sink. Store it in the same cans you melted it in. To clean pots and stirring tools, dip quickly in boiling water or run under very hot water. Immediately wipe clean with paper toweling.

• Dip wicking in wax for better burning and to keep from unraveling when inserting in wick hole.

• To poke wick hole, use hot knitting needle or #16 florist's wire instead of an ice pick.

• Level a finished candle by rotating it on a skillet over very low heat.

• Test colors in small glass jiggers—wax almost always dries lighter. (Use your samples for mini-candles—they'll have a marble-like gloss.)

• To release candle from a stubborn glass mold, put in refrigerator for half an hour.

• When melting down old candle stubs, fish out the blackened wicks with tongs.

• Warm glass molds in your hands or under hot water before adding wax.

• *To whip wax,* heat and then cool just to melting point. Beat in a shallow container with fork, eggbeater, or wire whisk.

• Remove coffee can rust rings from your good pans with scouring powder and steel wool.

• Cool glass container candles in a water bath at room temperature.

• Add white wax crayons or candle stubs to ordinary paraffin for greater whiteness and opacity.

• For evenly moistened sand, mix it well in a large roasting pan before pouring into smaller bowl.

• For well-packed sand, pound it with a wooden mallet.

• When making candles for dozens of friends or the church bazaar, pick *one* design and set up a production line. Leave enough time to do your own thing for your own home this Christmas!

# 17
# Plastic
# See-Throughs

Gay garden flowers decorate useful plastic coasters and trivets.

I hate even to mention plastic in this nature-loving book. To me, it's a dirty word. Besides, by this time plastic flower trivets are as common as, well, plastic. I include them here for several reasons. For one, as far as I'm concerned, I invented plastic trivets. For two, *anybody* can make better-looking see-throughs than the tacky daisy-and-fern creations sold everywhere. Thirdly, you can make them for a shadow of the ripoff retail price (say, one-twelfth). Mostly, I bring them up in case you think casting in plastic is a scary, highly specialized craft for experts only. It isn't.

When I·say I invented plastic trivets, I mean that I had never seen or heard of "liquid casting resin" five years ago. An art supply store sold it to me in lieu of what I had asked for—something to glue two sheets of Plexiglas together, my aim being to make a free-floating pressed flower picture without a frame. They didn't know any more about the crazy new stuff than

I, and the directions on the can were sketchy, to say the least, but, by-guess-and-by-golly, I finally got my free-floating pansies—plus a thousand other ideas to try with my newest glop. From plaques and trivets, it was a short step to shimmering mobiles and quickie coasters, which are still my own exclusives (I think).

Today, of course, there's no need to bumble around in the dark. There are booklets, classes, and whole departments in crafts shops devoted to the art of casting in plastic. But, as usual, I'll give you my own relaxed, non-expert methods and let you go on from there as you choose.

I should point out, regretfully, that this project isn't for everyone—apartment dwellers, for instance. For one thing, liquid plastic is smelly. It's hands down the most evil-smelling gunk in this book. Moreover, the fumes are unhealthy to inhale. You need plenty of ventilation, and you shouldn't work near food or, I should think, small children. You also need a room temperature of at least 70 degrees, with low humidity, and an absolutely level work surface. So, finding a spot to set up shop may be a problem, even for intrepid artisans with the most spacious homes.

## MATERIALS FOR CASTING IN PLASTIC

Clear Cast (or other liquid casting resin)
Catalyst (the hardening agent)
Molds (commercial or improvised)
Mold release
Stirring sticks (popsicle type)
Large paper cups
Small paper measuring cups
Tweezers
Pressed or dried materials

### OPTIONAL

Spray Glaze
Clear marbles
Glitter
Electric drill

## GENERAL DIRECTIONS FOR CASTING IN PLASTIC

Measure Clear Cast in small cup and pour into large cup. Add correct amount of catalyst carefully, drop by drop, according to the chart on the can. (Some experts

The basic casting ingredients

Measure Clear Cast in small cup and pour into large cup.

recommend using no more than 2 drops of catalyst per ounce of resin surrounding dried flowers.) Mix thoroughly for at least 1 minute. Pour into mold on level surface covered with newspapers. Glass molds must be pre-treated with mold release, and all molds will release castings more readily if pre-treated. Pour slowly to reduce air bubbles and prick any offenders with a pin. Pouring along and over the stirring stick will also help to reduce air bubbles.

When resin has begun to set but is still sticky or "tacky" on top (about 15 to 30 minutes), drop your dried flowers in place with tweezers. Remember that the down side of your casting may be the up side of your finished piece. Cover with another layer of resin, again removing air bubbles. (If you've misjudged on the depth of your layers, or just want a thicker casting, you can pour additional layers, of course.) Set casting aside to "cure" until it's "click hard"—anywhere from 2 hours to 2 days, depending upon the thickness, air temperature, humidity, and maybe just beginner's luck.

To unmold, a sharp tap may be all that is needed, but non-commercial molds are often temperamental. If your casting is stubborn, see the Tips at the end of the chapter.

## DIRECTIONS FOR FLOWER TRIVET

Spray a 5½-inch Pyrex dish with mold release. Add 4 ounces of catalyzed Clear Cast. When resin is tacky, add flowers. It's a good idea to plan intricate designs on paper first. Arrange the flowers and make a rough tracing, noting in which order overlapping materials must be placed to reproduce your design *in reverse* (the bottom of the dish will be the top of your trivet). Turn paper pattern over and retrace the lines in black so that you can see them through the dish placed on top. If you're simply strewing daisies and buttercups willy-nilly, just remember to put their best face *down*ward. Add "feet" to your trivet, if you like, by embedding 3 clear marbles. Cover with 4 more ounces of catalyzed resin, "cure" for at least 24 hours, and unmold. For a hanging plaque, drill hole and string by fishing line.

## DIRECTIONS FOR COASTERS

So far as I know, there are no ready-made molds for coasters. You could probably use plain round 3¾-inch plastic molds, but they're 89¢ apiece. I use 3¼-inch

Pouring over a stirring stick helps reduce air bubbles.

Arrange your flowers with tweezers.

Make a pattern showing where to place your arranged flowers.

Make feet for your trivet by inserting three marbles at the same time you insert your flowers.

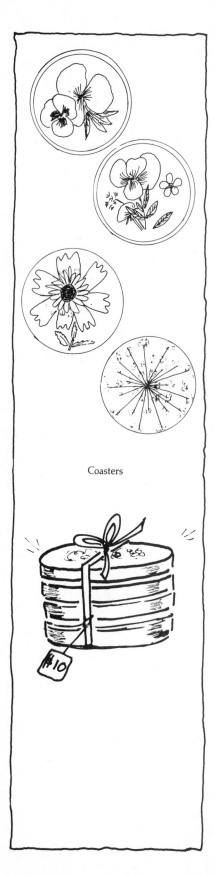

Coasters

metal lids that came with an old jelly-making set from the supermarket. Not only do my coasters turn out with rims but I can turn out a dozen at a time. For 12 coasters, mix about 6 ounces of Clear Cast. Be sure your first pour is shallow enough to leave room for the second. Add pressed flowers as soon as the surface is tacky (usually about 15 minutes). One nice thing about coasters is that the top side remains the top side—no brain strain involved in placing your flowers. Mix second pour, fill molds, and cure till click-hard. On a good day you might be able to unmold in an hour, but to be on the safe side, wait 24 hours.

All you really need are two pansies or a gay little mixed bouquet with foliage, or dream up your own flower, such as pulled-apart gaillardia petals with a daisy center. But, to me, there's nothing more elegant than one simple head of airy Queen Anne's lace (and you can whip up a dozen coasters, from start to finish, in a mere half-hour). Instead of coasters, drill holes for dangling disks to twinkle in a window—even one makes a respectable gift, especially if you embed a local wildflower for a relocated and homesick friend. Or you can preserve a favorite snapshot in your plaque.

P.S. I once brashly offered my coasters to the snootiest shop in town (fine jewelry, silver, and exclusive gifts). Amazingly, they agreed to sell all I could make—at $10 for a set of four (total cost to me about 10¢ apiece!). No, I never made my fortune. Typically, I ran out of pansies, or time, or sailed into some exciting new project. I never even got back to collect on my sample batch, but if any reader is looking for a quick and easy (if smelly) dollar . . .

## DIRECTIONS FOR MOBILE

Make castings in assorted glass and metal household molds. When click-hard, drill holes with electric drill and string from painted garden stakes.

The "butterflies" are flower petals that were taken apart and pressed individually—bright orange tithonia, hot pink zinnias, and blue delphinium, with various oddments for bodies and feelers (you have to press bulky blossoms like these petal by petal, anyway). A butterfly mobile takes longer than Queen Anne's lace coasters but actually, lethargy was the mother of this invention. I made it for a flower show rather than slave and sweat over a bona fide by-the-book bouquet. Not only did it win a ribbon (red, not blue) but I've still got *my* "arrangement." Considering that it's been

94

shimmering on our patio for five years, some of the flowers are still amazingly vivid (sunlight is death on dried flowers). It's also lived through thunder, lightning, rain, hailstones, and Hurricane Agnes. Tough stuff, this plastic, nasty word and all.

## TIPS ON CASTING IN LIQUID PLASTIC

• If high humidity causes tackiness, try putting the casting in the freezer in a sealed plastic bag for about 15 minutes.
• Smooth rough outside edges of casting with fine sandpaper.
• For an extra-glassy surface, spray with Spray Glaze. You can also rejuvenate old stained or cloudy coasters and trivets with Spray Glaze.
• For extra glamour, add gold glitter to your resin.
• You can also color Clear Cast. Use transparent or opaque dye, pearl luster, luminous or gold pigment, available in hobby shops.
• Try coloring just the last background pour of a trivet; then you can glue on a felt base instead of embedding glass "feet."
• For a more dimensional effect, embed two or three layers of materials in separate pours.
• Depending on the thickness of the casting, you can embed 3-dimensional flowers and other treasures as well as pressed flowers.
• If casting is stubborn to unmold, run it under very hot water, then cold water.
• If a glass or metal casting is *impossible* to unmold, I place it in a 200-degree oven, then in the freezer. You may have to do this more than once, but *don't give up.* Return to oven briefly to remove any cloudiness.
• Consult your hobby shop or the many pamphlets available if you have further questions or want to learn the finer points of plastic casting.
• Remember that there are no hard-and-fast formulae for success. What works for you one day may not the next—depending upon the air temperature, humidity, amount of catalyst, age of catalyst, how long you stir, size of your mold, size of your embedment, et cetera. But don't worry—*all* plastic castings will harden eventually.

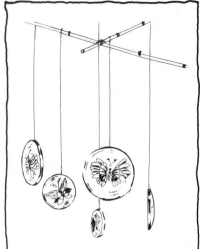

My "Butterflies Are Free" mobile

# 18
# Velvet
# Saint Nick

I don't often pay $5 for an ornament, one single solitary Christmas ornament. In fact, I won't pay a nickel for anything I think I can trot home and make myself. That was the trouble with this irresistibly old-worldly sourpuss of a Santa with his gold-rimmed specs and velvet cap. At first blush, I thought he was out of my league and I had no choice but to dig in my wallet like any other Christmas shopper.

I'm not sorry I did, as it turns out. At second glance, he didn't look nearly so impossible to tackle. (You'll find that's true of many decorations, and having a sample in hand is well worth your initial

Velvet Saint Nick

investment—you can go on to turn out fifty of them for $5.) After all, what was he but a scrap of velvet, some drugstore cotton, and a twist of wire? And that face, of course. But that was no problem, I thought. Why not snip a face out of some old Christmas card or magazine? I'll tell you why not—because there are no old-fashioned, unsmiling St. Nicholases with piercing aquamarine eyes and jutting aquiline noses around these days. All you can find are jolly, apple-cheeked, red-nosed roly-polies on skis and surf boards, alas. You may have better luck than I did, but you'll probably have to draw your own face. Here's a sample sketch to guide you, but don't worry too much about making a perfect copy—believe me, the bifocals and beard help a lot. In fact, don't worry if the whole project drives you dingy—to me, it's the *hardest* thing in the book.

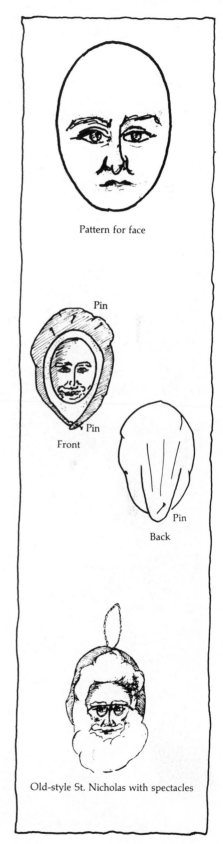

Pattern for face

Front

Back

Old-style St. Nicholas with spectacles

## MATERIALS FOR VELVET SAINT NICK

3-inch styrofoam egg
Triangle of velvet or velveteen approximately
    8 by 7 by 7 inches
Cotton batting (or cotton cosmetic balls or jewelry box
    liners)
3- to 4-inch piece of thin wire
Watercolors
Shellac
Straight pins
Elmer's glue

## DIRECTIONS FOR VELVET SAINT NICK

Draw and paint face. Cut out and glue to styrofoam egg (take a slice off the front of the egg for easier gluing). Shellac face (or coat with plastic spray or Mod Podge). Pin velvet triangle around egg; fold neatly in back and pin at base. Glue cotton to egg for fur, hair, and beard, covering all pins. Add ball of cotton to tip of cap. Twist shiny gold or silver wire into spectacles and poke into egg. Finish off with a sprig of green felt or ribbon "holly" pinned on with red sequin "berries." Attach hanging string with straight pin (thin gold metal chain is more elegant).

   Of course, you can make larger or smaller Saint Nicks. My extravagant $5 import was only half this size. And, if you don't have any scraps of velvet handy, you might invest in rich burgundy-red silk velvet, like the original.

# 19
# Kitchen-Jar
# Candlesticks

Opulent jumbo candlesticks from humble materials

The butcher, the baker, the . . . who, you? *You* make candlesticks like this elegant, opulent, white-and-gold two-footer? Why not? A twelve-year-old can do it. I'll admit that when I saw my first jumbo candlestick under the tree one memorable Christmas morning, I couldn't believe it was the loving creation of our sixth-grade daughter. But that will give you an idea of the elementary how-to's and inexpensive what-with's required (also an idea of the wonders wrought by our elementary school art teachers; our house is filled with money-can't-buy-'em treasures inspired by Mrs. Dorothy Cecil, and for this one I thank her especially).

Here's your chance to empty your kitchen closets and basement of all that accumulated junk. Recycle those mustard, mayonnaise, pickle, jam, and peanut butter jars. Round up all those coffee, juice, soup, and tuna fish cans. Are you a string saver? Good—you can use that, too. In fact, you can even put yesterday's newspapers to work. (If you haven't papier-mâchéd since your own grammar-school days, I'll refresh your memory.)

Copy the designs here, if you like, but you'll have more fun thinking up your own. And you don't have to stick to Christmasy white and gold. To tell the truth, I like my daughter's first try better than any I've seen since. Hers is deep, dark midnight blue, but after nine years, it's turned a little camera-shy. Other good choices are muted Williamsburg shades of old gold, burnt apricot, or soft green, especially if you antique your candlestick. But try high-gloss orange or kelly green, if that's more your style.

The silvery candlestick is almost embarrassingly elementary. I include it mostly to goad you into outshining the teacher. All it takes is a tin can, a glass jar, and an old toothbrush (to spatter with).

## MATERIALS FOR PAPIER-MÂCHÉ CANDLESTICK

Assorted household jars and cans
Old china saucers
Paper toweling or newspapers
Wheat paste
String or cord
Spray enamel
Radiator paint, gold or silver
Elmer's glue or Weldit cement

Various string designs; you'll think up many others.

99

## DIRECTIONS FOR PAPIER-MÂCHÉ CANDLESTICK

Experiment with your jars, cans, and saucers to find the best-looking, best-balanced lineup (you can invert them, too, of course). Only glass jars are used in the candlestick shown, but jumbo ringed juice cans are perfect for this project (although they may rust through the papier-mâché in time). Glue jars in place and let dry for 30 minutes. Glue sections A and B separately; it's much easier to papier-mâché and trim your candlestick in sections. Also, note that saucers are *not* papier-mâchéd, to prevent tippiness.

While waiting for the glue to dry, plan your cording design, mentally or on paper. The idea is to be ready to decorate as soon as you've finished papier-mâchéing. Cord dipped in wheat paste sticks nicely to wet papier-mâché. You can use any ordinary household twine, but braided Venetian blind cord or indoor clothesline is better. First, plan the horizontal lines, following the natural indentations of your jars. Next, plan the areas in between, filling in with squiggles, loops, stripes, or whatever.

To papier-mâché your candlestick, mix wheat paste according to the directions on the package. The consistency should be something like good gravy or thinnish vichyssoise. Tear (don't cut) paper toweling or newspaper into strips about 1 inch wide and 9 inches long. Dip into paste, running your fingers down each strip to remove excess paste and lumps. Apply strips in random crisscrosses until entire surface is covered. Gently smooth out finished section with clean, moistened fingertips. (By this time, you'll either be a papier-mâché pro or have thrown up your gooey hands in disgust. Of course, if you're an old hand at the art, by all means use your own favorite technique.)

Now you're ready to decorate. Measure and cut cording into lengths desired. Allow a little extra for shrinkage. Saturate cord in paste and press firmly in place. Set aside to dry, preferably overnight. When candlestick is dry, repair any loose cords with Elmer's glue.

Glue dried sections together and spray paint desired color. (I sprayed my candle flat white with a top coat of clear plastic because I didn't have enamel. The name of the game in any craft is—improvise.) Dry thoroughly. Gild cord carefully with small artist's brush. Dust saucers lightly with gold spray, masking off surrounding area. For antique effect, rub on silver or gold paint with cheesecloth.

Glue sections A and B separately. Use pill bottle at top for candle holder.

Spatter paint by scraping knife *toward* you over toothbrush.

## DIRECTIONS FOR SILVER CANDLESTICK

Pile up any combination of tin cans and glass jars; cement together. Spatter paint at random by scraping knife over toothbrush dipped in silver paint. Note: draw knife *toward* you or you'll end up with more silver on you than on the candlestick. Spatter painting gives a more subtle effect than spray painting and is easier to control.

## TIPS ON MAKING CANDLESTICKS

• Instead of pressing cord trim into wet papier-mâché, you can glue gilded cord onto finished candle. It's a matter of naming your poison. Hand-gilding the cord is a painstaking job, but so is gluing it on.
• Prepare a whole batch of papier-mâché strips at a time; drape them over your mixing pan. You'll save a lot of time and trouble rinsing off your lumpy, dumpy fingers.
• Use the easy-mix variety of papier-mâché available in art stores, if you're lazy.
• Dorothy Cecil recommends unbleached paper toweling for the smoothest surface. Heavy, good-quality toweling requires only one layer; thinner stuff may require two.
• Remember that it's risky to papier-mâché your saucers. Papier-mâché shrinks and you may end up with a tippy candlestick.
• When pressing wet cord onto wet candlestick, it will help to lay the candlestick on its side, in any way you can devise.
• Remember to cut cording pieces *longer* than you need. Some cord shrinks and you'll begin to think you need new glasses.
• *Plan* your design; don't have squiggles and swirls just floating in thin air.
• Instead of Elmer's glue, use household epoxy for greater durability. Weldit cement works well if you score the metal first.
• For an extra-fancy candlestick, glue on at the base any of the other decorative make-it-yourselfs in the book—gilded salt dough roses, pine cone flowers, seashell ornaments, et cetera.
• Have a good time. Don't fret if your candlestick falls somewhat short of perfection. Who wants one that looks as if it came out of a mold in Ceramics 100?

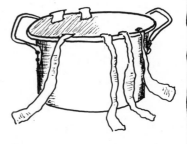

Drape papier-mâché over edge of pan to make application easier.

# 20
# Calico
# Bow Wreath

Christmas-bright calico wreath—no sewing required!

A few years ago, *House Beautiful* flaunted a wreath like this on the cover of their traditionally fat and fabulous Christmas issue. Their wreath was made of expensive ribbon, was designed by a flossy New York City florist, and, as the editors kindly warned their readers, took *five hours* to make. This charming country cousin of *HB*'s city-slicker is made of strips of bargain-counter calico that are simply twisted into quickie bows and tacked on with jiffy straight pins. Even the slowest poke couldn't slave away for five hours.

You'll find dozens of bright-eyed prints, checks, and polka dots at the five-and-ten and in fabric shops (check the remnant counters first) for less than $1 a yard. For an even thriftier wreath, use your own left-overs, if you're a home sewer. Or how about recycling

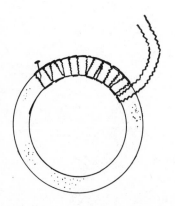

If you're sentimental, use pieces of favorite cast-offs to make your bows.

To cover styrofoam, secure the end of a strip of fabric with a pin, and wrap around and around.

those cast-off kitchen curtains or old printed sheets? For a truly nostalgic keepsake wreath, snip up your daughter's and your own old pet frocks that you're too sentimental to part with but never take out of their storage boxes.

Instead of a gaudy crazy-quilt wreath, try a more subtle, sophisticated version. Combine baby blue, pink, and brown gingham checks—or black-and-white polka dots, gray glen plaid, and white eyelet—or all different shades and patterns of green fabrics. And, if you want to gild the lily, you can wire on or pin on all sorts of trims—tiny, shiny plastic bags of herbs, pine cones, Christmas balls, dried flowers, fake fruits, or, for the children's room, miniature figures and toys. *Wreath shown courtesy of Mrs. John C. (Emily) Ulrich.*

## MATERIALS FOR CALICO BOW WREATH

14-inch styrofoam ring
⅓ yard each of 5 different cotton prints (For one wreath, you need only 11 inches of 36-inch-wide fabric, if your fabric store will oblige. If you must buy a full yard, look for 44- to 46-inch-wide fabrics—just right for four wreaths.)
¼ yard more of any of the 5 prints, to cover base and make dangling bow
Straight pins
Pinking shears

## DIRECTIONS FOR CALICO BOW WREATH

### TO COVER WREATH

From ¼ yard piece of fabric, cut with pinking shears 2 strips 2 by 36 inches (or 2 by 45 inches, if that's the width of your fabric). Pin end of first strip to styrofoam ring and wrap around and around. Secure with pin and continue with second strip until entire wreath is covered; pin.

### TO MAKE BOWS

From each ⅓ yard of fabric, cut 24 pinked strips 1½ by 11 inches long (sorry, bows will not work with 12-inch-long strips). Don't be frazzled by the directions and diagrams—they look more complicated than they are. Once you've mastered your first bow, you'll toss off the rest in seconds.

To start bow, fold the strip over on the right side of the fabric about 3 inches from the end (Figure 1). Cross strip over to form a point (Figure 2). Bring other end toward this point, with right side of fabric still up, to form matching point (Figure 3); slip end inside first point. Insert pin in center, thus catching both ends of strip (Figure 4). Side view, bow will look like Figure 5.

## TO MAKE WREATH

Pin bows to wreath as close together as possible. Alternate your colors and prints, as well as the angle of your bows. Cover inner and outer rims well, too, but leave the back plain to rest flat against the wall or door. Leave room at lower right to pin on a large dangling double-faced bow. To make bow, cut remainder of ¼ yard fabric into 2 long 3-inch-wide strips. Line up with wrong sides facing in and tie into bow. Loop thin wire around the top of wreath to hang.

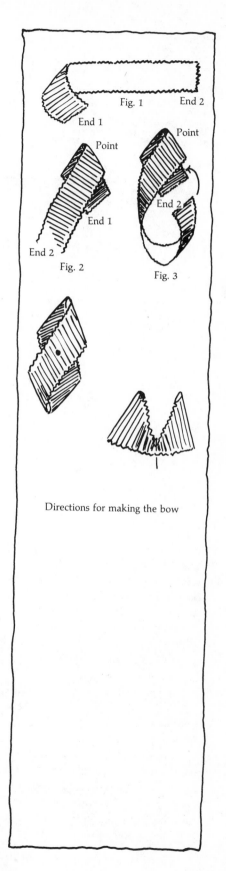

Directions for making the bow

# 21
# Recycled
# Wrappings

A handful of ideas for merry, money-saving recycled wrappings

I come from a long line of wrap-happy souls who firmly believe 'tis more blessed to wrap than to receive. For years, I'm sure I spent more on fabulous papers, fancy ribbon, exquisite trims, and elegant tags than I did on the presents inside. Cheerfully, blissfully. After all, that's what Christmas was all about. But then came the crunch. Suddenly, what Christmas, and the world, was all about was Economy, Ecology, the Environment.

So, farewell to inch-thick golden foils, real silk velvet ribbon, white satin roses, and 50¢ coordinated gift tags. Obviously, it was time to reform, retrench, recycle, improvise, make do. On with the old and off with the new! Well, a funny thing happened on the way to the flea market—I discovered that wrapping was more fun than ever and I haven't set foot in Norcross country since. Here are some ideas for wrapping *your* most beautiful presents ever for the least money ever, and loving every noble, martyred minute of it.

# PAPER WRAPPINGS

Kids are natural artists.

Even grown-ups can doodle a tree.

Block printing with a potato

Use your wallpaper remnants.

Even at your friendly gas station, rolls of gift wrap cost too much. Besides, poinsettias and yellow lanterns on a royal blue ground are ugly. If you want to buy paper by the roll, get yourself a jumbo roll of shelf paper—the shiny white good-quality stuff. Then turn the whole family loose with a set of Magic Markers—including Mom and Dad. The kids, of course, will outshine you with all kinds of gay and amusing doodles, but even the most inhibited, non-arty grown-up can come up with an okay Christmas tree or bough of holly. And you may surprise yourself.

If you want to get fancy, draw on your designs with Elmer's glue and sprinkle them with glitter. Or try spatter painting for a confetti effect or a stenciled design. Then there's what they call "crackle and dip." Wet down a good grade of white paper and crumple it well. Lay flat and paint the entire surface with watercolor; rinse under faucet and let dry. The paint will remain in the creases.

Remember block-printing with a potato in grammar school? It works swell on shelf paper. Slice a fresh potato and carve out your design at least ¼ inch deep. Dip in poster paint.

Another good bet is wallpaper, especially if you have scads of presents to wrap and like the coordinated look. You probably have odd rolls of your own lying around the attic, but you can always find bargain-priced leftovers in the wallpaper shops. You'll be surprised how many wallpaper patterns are downright Christmasy, if you stretch your imagination. You could certainly use a merry red Provincial print or a leafy green-and-white, or anything that's gilded, flocked or brocaded. You may find wallpaper a little tricky at first, especially at the corners, but you'll soon get the hang of it. Speaking of which, the newer self-adhesive papers might be a lot easier. I've never tried them, but they're probably like Con-Tact—easy when you know how. (The main trouble with Con-Tact is the price, and you seldom run into remnants.)

The best papers of all are not only cheap—they're free. Such as old newspapers. How about wrapping Dad's gift in his beloved sports section or the financial page (tuck a pleated dollar bill into the bow—you know *that* will be recycled)? For the kids, use comic strips; for a teen-age daughter, a fashion ad; for Grandma, the gardening page; for Auntie, the crossword puzzle. Old magazine covers are even more glossy and colorful; so are seed catalogues, old football programs, you name it. Make a game out of Christmas morning opening—skip the tags so that everybody has to guess whose gift is whose by the cover.

Are you the kind who saves a few favorite papers from the fire each year? Surprise your sentimental teen-age daughter with a patchwork present made of papers that go back to when she really believed in Santa Claus. Patchwork wrappings are a good way to use up all your old small scraps—also the best way to handle huge problem boxes.

Before we go any further, do you know the first rule of gift-wrapping? You don't cover the *whole* box— you cover only the lid. It saves on paper; it saves all that unwrapping mess all over the floor; and, of course, it saves your hand-painted "work of art" for posterity (or, anyway, next year). Did you know that the artistic director of Henri Bendel in New York suggests using Kraft paper for your Christmas package artwork? The paper is durable enough to be framed later. Says he, "Wrappings are as much a part of the gift as the gift. Choose them carefully, so they can be recycled in another person's life." Needless to say, I say, "Amen."

But I should warn you of one large built-in danger of do-it-yourself gift-wrapping. When you've put time and thought and "you" into a package, instead of mere filthy lucre, you may suddenly care about how people open it. You may turn into a "peeler-offer" instead of a "ripper." You'll want to scream when family or friends tear into your package tooth-and-nail. But don't. Assuming that your effort isn't *really* framable, remember that it cost you nothing, you had fun doing it, and you can always top yourself next year.

Here's a nifty paper solution for awkward, oddly shaped presents without boxes—paper bags. Even plain brown supermarket bags can be dressed up, but colored or white bakery bags are prettier. Decorate them with Magic Markers; fringe or scallop the tops; add fancy yarn or ribbon handles. East House (15 East 22nd Street, New York, New York 10010) makes super-gay, super-sturdy bags that can be used over and over.

Once you start looking for thrifty new ideas, you'll find them everywhere. One of my pet papers looks like a splashy abstract painting, and it is—sort of. It's what happens when you cover a palette of gloppy oils with cellophane to keep the paints from drying and then pick it up. Pure serendipity. (Allow plenty of time for the cellophane to dry, or place it face down on another sheet of solid-color paper.) I've since heard that you can also float oil paints on water, swirl them around, and drop a piece of paper flat on the surface for another one-of-a-kind luxury paper.

Tuck a pleated dollar bill into a bow.

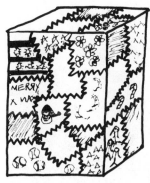

A patchwork present made of yester-Yule scraps

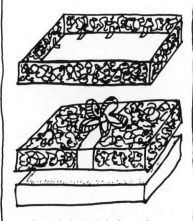

Cover only the lid of your box.

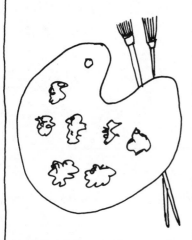

Scallop the top of a paper bag.

You'll find thrifty new ideas everywhere.

Nothing looks more expensive than fabric wrappings.

## FABRIC WRAPPINGS

As you've seen, there's nothing tacky about using wrappings more than once. Which brings us to my favorite wrapping of all—real, honest, Fruit-of-the-Loom, all-cotton-and-a-yard-wide fabric. Nothing looks more expensive. Even the fanciest number at the luxury gift-wrap counter can't hold a candle to a package swathed in baby-blue gingham or tomato-red burlap or rich green velvet. But the truth is your own fabric-wrapped packages are cheaper. In fact, fabric is one of the thriftiest wrappings there is. How much can one quarter yard of even a luxury fabric cost? And you can use it over and over, year after year. Even the most wild-eyed unwrapper can't rip it to shreds. What's more, you can save a lot of money on ribbon. From a yard of pretty fabric you can cut miles of streamers with pinking shears to tie into extravagant, elegant matching bows.

Wrapping with fabric is just as easy as wrapping with paper. Ordinary Scotch tape will hold your package together. Instead of covering just the lid, as with paper, I usually wrap the whole box. That way you have a big piece to use again next year. Or you can "upholster" your box more or less permanently by gluing on the fabric (brush the entire surface with diluted Elmer's) or by tacking it on with a staple gun. This is an especially good idea for shallow-lidded boxes that need their bottoms covered too. Even cheapie garden-supply burlap looks chic this way; pin on a corsage of dried flowers and grasses.

If you're a home sewer, you probably have yards of remnants lying around the house, many of them perfect for Christmas wrapping—gay calicoes, dainty florals, red-and-white checks, white cotton eyelet, bright green sailcloth. But don't be a stick-in-the-mud traditionalist. What's wrong with black-and-white polka dots, brown plaid, or abstract prints in crazy colors? You've probably noticed that exclusive boutiques love offbeat wrappings; in fact, the snootier the shop, the wilder the shopping bag. And use every scrap of your precious velvet remnants, whatever the color. It only takes a tiny square to wrap a teensy jewelry or perfume box in splendor. When big presents come in small packages, they might as well *look* big, no?

Non-sewers, like myself, can have even more fun. Here's your chance to root and rummage through the remnant counters like your domestic sisters. And you'll probably have them to yourself because who has time to sew in December? You'll find mountains of tempting leftovers at beautiful bargain prices, and you never know what goodie you'll unbury. Could you resist a Raggedy Ann print with candy canes and holly at 50 percent off? I couldn't. And by luck I had a handmade Raggedy Ann ornament on hand to top off the package. Even if you don't have matching fabric, a doll-face ornament makes a saucy trim. Use an old silver ball; glue on colored yarn for hair and plastic eyes from a crafts shop; paint features with red and black Magic Markers. *Courtesy of Betsy Church.*

## DOUBLE-DUTY WRAPPINGS

Instead of fabric remnants, how about tying up your gift in a colorful cotton bandana? That way your wrapping becomes really a second present. Bandana prints come in dozens of colors now, besides the old faithful red and navy, but the prices are still hobo-style. Or use a lacy white all-girl handkerchief. Along the same lines, a pretty box that can be put to good use later is all the wrapping you need. Look for decorated metal tea cannisters, English biscuit boxes, or cake tins. Also with the future in mind, why not wrap with scented lingerie drawer liners?

## RIBBONS AND TIES

You already know about cutting your own ribbon to match your fabric packages. Use pinked fabric ribbon for other packages, too—it's cheaper than almost any other you can buy. Are you crazy about the new stiffened ribbon they sell in florists' and crafts shops? You can make your own by bonding Stitch Witchery to your fabric before cutting it into strips.

Actually, any real, old-fashioned satin or grosgrain ribbon is a better buy in the long run than one-shot paper ribbon. But, if you're strictly a member of the throwaway generation, at least buy your paper ribbon shrewdly. Don't throw your money away on the smallest spools of the widest ribbon—the ones that are always featured at the ribbon counter. Check the yardage and be sure you get the most ribbon for your money. And do you really need ribbon that wide? The best buy on the shelves is a jumbo roll of narrow ¼-inch ribbon. In fact, I like skinny, hair-line gold string—the kind you find mostly in crafts shops (50 yards, not feet, for about $1). Do you remember when department stores used to gift wrap every package with "good stuff"? One of the most elegant ties was

Use un-Christmasy patterns.

Wrap a tiny "big" present in velvet splendor.

Raggedy Ann, dressed for Christmas

Bandanna wrapping is a second present.

A pretty tea caddy

You can recycle shiny plastic bags

. . . and leftover name tapes.

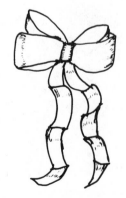

A fancy bow with wired streamers

Lord & Taylor's gold roping. Try making your own by dipping household twine in gold paint.

You probably have other "ribbon" around the house that you've never thought of using. Save the cellophane that comes between dressmaker ribbons and trims on the spool—it has a nice sparkle. I've even recycled the plastic bags that newspapers come in on rainy days into shimmery, giant-sized bows. How about the miles of name tags that you never sewed into the kids' camp clothes? How about Dad's old narrow silk ties? Glue on ball fringe and other decorator trims to outline a package.

Be stingy with the ribbon you've got. Tie a package only in the middle, or the long way, or on the diagonal. *Don't* tie it—use just a bow. That's another good reason for wrapping just the top of your box—it uses less ribbon. Tape it down along with your wrapping paper inside the lid.

A word on bows. I've already described how to wire a bow the garden-club way on page 31. You'll find that wired bows come in especially handy when you're gift wrapping. The wires also make it easy to add trims to your bow. Here's a more advanced wiring trick. To make a rippled satin or velvet bow, cut 2 pieces of ribbon for each streamer. Place a length of wire between them and glue together. Coax the streamers into glamorous curves and fasten to the top bow. Taped to a long, skinny package, it's all the decoration you need.

## TRIMS AND SUCH

You don't even need ribbon, if you're clever with your trimmings. Let's hope that, for starters, you already have a goodly supply of goodies squirreled away. I don't mean faded plastic poinsettias or tired old paper rosettes, but trims that are worth saving and reusing, like Santa Clauses, bells, snowmen, glass baubles, velvet roses, and the like. Such trinkets can become a part of your family's Christmas tradition. By all means, splurge on a few new irresistibles each year—*after* Christmas, when they're even more irresistible at 50 percent off.

But how about some less conventional trims? Let's start with a few that you *can't* save year after year, like edibles. Have you ever thought of a fresh juicy orange as a Christmas trim? Take a tip from the Europeans, who still make fruit a part of their holiday festivities. Wrap an orange, apple, or cluster of smaller fruits in shiny plastic; tuck in a sprig of greenery or a few nuts.

For a family sweet tooth, slip a pretty miniature box of chocolates under your bow. Of course, cellophane-wrapped candy canes are always good; so are wrapped sourballs or other hard candies wired into colorful clusters.

Then there are fresh greens, to me the poshest trims going. But don't run to the florist for holly, mistletoe, and magnolia leaves. Raid your own backyard. The lowliest evergreen will do—privet, pine, or yew. Even better are boxwood, Japanese holly (the poor girl's boxwood), blue cedar, aucuba, euonymus, Chinese holly, or what have you. Just tuck a few dewy sprays into a red bow and your decorating is done. (Condition greens overnight by sprinkling with water and sealing in a plastic bag.)

Along with your greens, or by themselves, there's nothing like nuts, cones, and pods that you've gathered yourself. Wire them for easier handling and be sure to glamorize some with gold spray and glitter. Deodar cedar cones make gorgeous roses, and other cones can be sliced into pretty flowers (see Chapter 5). Honey locust pods can be gilded to look just like golden ribbons. Just as is, lance eucalyptus looks like silvery ribbon.

Dried flowers are another bright thought. If you have precious, fragile specimens like daffodils, glue them to the top of your box and cover with plastic wrap. (Does that sound more like an Easter present to you? To me, it isn't Christmas without a pot of fragrant forced paperwhite narcissus in bloom.) But little jiffy bouquets tucked into your bow are just as appealing. The best flowers to use are, happily, the easiest ones to dry—baby's breath, yarrow, goldenrod, and artemesia—all of which can be air-dried by hanging upside down on a clothesline or hanger in a dark place. Spray them gold or silver if you like. And this is one time when even cheap plastic flowers are OK to use. You can turn the worst-looking five-and-ten rose into a long-stemmed beauty with gold spray and glitter.

You'll find other ideas for trims scattered throughout the book. How about a corn husk angel or a milkweed pod poinsettia? How about a seashell flower or a twinkly tin can star?

## GIFT TAGS

Tags are probably the most foolish waste of your Christmas dollars. Do you really need those run-of-the-mill stringed tags in cellophane packs at 25¢ or 50¢

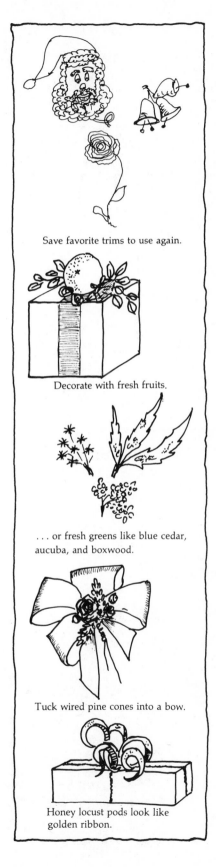

Save favorite trims to use again.

Decorate with fresh fruits.

. . . or fresh greens like blue cedar, aucuba, and boxwood.

Tuck wired pine cones into a bow.

Honey locust pods look like golden ribbon.

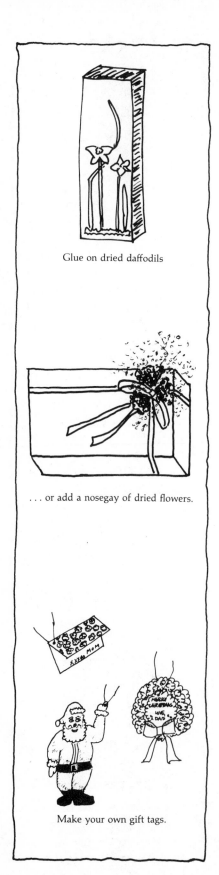

Glue on dried daffodils

. . . or add a nosegay of dried flowers.

Make your own gift tags.

a throw (and thrown they will be, lickety-split)? If you want to coordinate your tags to your wrappings, there's a better way. Simply cut off a snip of the gift paper and fold it over. Or why not put all those old Christmas cards to work? Even if you only have last year's batch to look through, you'll probably find just the right holly wreath or jolly Santa or red rose to go with your wrapping. Cut it out, poke a hole, and add a string. Cut up all those elegant thick gold cards, too, into simple rectangles and squares. Are you mailing a gift to friends out of town? Cut your tag from *their* card last year—they'll remember it, all right, and be dumbfounded that anyone else did.

How about reusing last year's tags, just within the family, that is? When I come across oldies that say "To Dad, love and kisses, Santa" or "Merry, merry to Cyn from Mom," I've been known to push them through a second time. Most old tags survive accidentally, but there are always a few I save for sentimental reasons. My daughter dug up one such—an especially love-y her-to-me tag that I couldn't bear to throw out—and added a shiny new twist to our recycling game. She tacked on a "P. S. and even more so *this* year."

Thinking up your own tags makes *un*-wrapping more fun, too. It shouldn't all be over in one hectic half hour. One way to stretch it out is to write your *to's* and *from's* in the form of riddles. (This is an especially good trick if you're an early wrapper and want to keep your "peekers" busy with enigmatic clues.) You might even write your riddles in rhymed couplets. Try it—it doesn't have to be immortal Shakespearean verse. I've already suggested wrapping your gifts in "guess-who?" recycled papers, in which case you don't need tags at all. And, of course, you'll include the message in all your hand-doodled works of art.

## RECYCLED PRESENTS

To wrap up the whole subject of wrapping and recycling, have you ever thought of giving your loved ones a nice, *used* present? I don't mean putting a new bow on Billy's old rubber duck or trying again with the tie that Dad's only worn once all year. I mean wrapping up, for your English major son, a precious set of Dickens that his grandmother gave to his grandfather. I mean presenting your teen-age daughter with a favorite childhood volume that your mother gave *you* one long-ago Christmas, or a piece of her great-aunt's jewelry. True, these are gifts that would come their way anyway, in due time. True, you have to know your children—hand-me-downs instead of new hi-fi's won't be everybody's cup of Christmas cheer. But, what with the new generation's concern for the environment, contempt for commercialism, and love for telling-it-like-it-is, your offspring might even think your idea is neat. A little flaky, but neat.

What can you lose? At least, it's something else for them to unwrap, and for *you* to have fun wrapping.

Could it be blue-flowered notepaper?

Hand-painted presents need no tag.

# Index

Linoleum paste, 6, 17, 20, 26, 35-36
Loblolly cones, 25, 30
Love-in-a-mist, 73
Lubin, Charles, Company, 3
*Lunaria*, 30, 31

Macaroni
 "flowers," 21
 mirror, 18-21
 shapes, 17
 tree, 16-17
Madonna, 12
Magnolia leaf daisy, 79-81
Maia, Ronaldo (florist), 3
Marbles, 8, 92-93
Marzipan, 48
Mexican star, 57
Milkweed pods, 74, 75, 78
Miniature wreaths, 34-39
Mobile, plastic, 94-95
Mod Podge, 6, 97
Money plant *(Lunaria)*, 30, 31
Mouse ornament, 47, 48

Nature flowers, 76-81
Nature ornaments, 72-75
Newspaper wrappings, 108
Notepaper, 40-43
Nuts, 25, 37, 38

Oasis (floral foam), 4
Okra pods, 75
O'Neill, Cynthia Lamb, 70, 75
Oyster shell ornament, 74

Package trims, 112-113
Paper bags, 109
Paper wrappings, 108-109
Papier-mâché, 6-7, 13, 68, 100
Paraffin, 33, 85. *See also* Wax
Parsley, 41
Patchwork wrappings, 109
Patterns
 angel, corn husk, 74
 angel, tin, 59
 bird, papier-mâché, 71
 bird, tin, 59
 butterfly, tin, 60
 calico bow, 105
 candlestick, 100
 egg carton ornaments, 69
 envelope, 43
 fish, tin, 60
 golden angel wing, 14
 pinwheel, tin, 59

 Saint Nick, 97
 stars, 56, 57, 71
Patterson, Mrs. William A., 75
Peach pits, 24, 35
Pegboard, 24
Peony, corn husk, 79
Pier One (store), 3
Pine cones
 "flowers," 25, 27, 28-31
 kindling basket, 32-33
 miniature wreaths, 34-39
 plaque, 24, 26
 preparation of, 25
 suppliers, 7
 varieties of, 24-26
 wiring of, 25
 wreaths, 22-27
Pinholders, 4, 52, 53
Piñon cones, 23, 24-25, 30
Pinwheel ornament, 58, 59
Pistachios, 22, 35, 37, 38
Plastic balls, 7, 73
Plastic casting, 90-95
 coasters, 93
 general directions, 92-93
 mobile, 94
 supplies, 7-8, 92
 tips on, 95
 trivet, 93
Plastic see-throughs, 90-95
Pod Happy Shop, The, 3
Pods, 24, 26, 74-75
Poinsettia, 76, 78
Polyurethane varnish, 8, 48
Potato printing, 108
Pressing flowers, 40-41
Princeton University, 41
Prune pits, 24, 36, 39

Queen Anne's lace, 23, 75, 94
Quickie (floral foam), 4

Raggedy Ann, 111
Radiator paint, 8, 99
Recycled wrappings, 106-115
Redwood cones, 25, 30, 38
Rex brand wheat paste, 9
Ribbon and bead ornaments, 68-69
Ribbons and ties, 68, 110-112. *See also* Bows
Rose hips , 30
Rose petals, 35
Roses
 candle, 88
 deodar cedar. *Which see.*